AFRICAN
MYTHS & LEGENDS

✳   ✳   ✳

For Jacinta

First published in Great Britain by Brockhampton Press, a member of the Hodder Headline Group,
20 Bloomsbury Street, London WC1B 3QA.

ISBN 1 86019 367 6

A copy of the CIP data is available from the British Library upon request.

Created and produced by Flame Tree Publishing, a part of The Foundry Creative Media Company Limited,
The Long House, Antrobus Road, Chiswick, London W4 5HY.

AFRICAN
Myths & Legends

O. B. DUANE

CONTENTS

INTRODUCTION

AFRICA IS A VAST CONTINENT, over three times the size of the United States of America, incorporating a huge expanse of desert and scrubland, mountains, valleys, rain forests, swamps, rivers and lakes. For much of its history, however, a large part of southern Africa has remained cut off from the outside world. The Sahara Desert, which divides the north from the south, covers nearly one-third of the continent, presenting an almost impossible obstacle for even the most resilient traveller.

North Africa stretches from Morocco to Egypt, and down through the Nile valley as far as Ethiopia. This rich and fertile region nurtures a distinctly Mediterranean culture dominated by Muslim and Christian religions. Africa south of the Sahara – the area known as 'Negro' or 'Black' Africa from which the myths and legends of this book have been selected – extends from the east and west Sudan, down through the savannas and central rain forests right into South Africa.

Sub-Saharan Africa is a land of colourful contrasts and diverse cultures, many of which have existed for hundreds and even thousands of years. Europeans remained ignorant of the region's rich history until the fifteenth century when the Portuguese arrived on the west coast, landing at the Cape of Good Hope. Before long, they were transporting thousands of African slaves to Europe and the Americas, a lucrative trade that continued until the mid-nineteenth century.

During the late nineteenth century, white settlers, among them the French, English and Dutch, began to explore further inland, and throughout the 1880s and 1890s they competed furiously for ownership of territories rich in natural resources, carving up the continent between them. By 1900, almost all of Africa was in European hands, remaining under European control until the 1950s, when the colonies began to demand their independence.

Archaeological research has revealed that by about 1200 BC, rich and powerful civilizations, such as that of Ancient Egypt, had developed in the northern part of Africa. Nothing now remains of these impressive empires, but their customs and beliefs are well recorded. Relatively little is known, on the other hand, of the earliest history of the peoples living south of the Sahara. Geographical isolation dictated that these peoples developed largely by themselves. Written culture became widespread only in the nineteenth century; before that time, the art of writing was completely unknown to Africans in the equatorial forests and the south.

The radical changes forced on the African continent as a result of colonialism and the slave trade led to the destruction of many traditional societies which had evolved over the centuries. Much information on Africa's cultural heritage remains buried forever, since there are no ancient books or documents to enlighten us. But Africa has always had a powerful tradition of storytelling. Before a European way of life prevailed, the old religions, rules and customs provided the raw material for those tribesmen who first promoted this extremely colourful oral culture.

Opposite:
White settlers began to explore further inland, and throughout the 1880s and 1890s they competed furiously for land rich in natural resources.

African people have persevered with their storytelling and continue to leave records of their history in songs and stories they pass down from parent to child through the generations. Stories are commonly told in the evening when the day's work is done, accompanied by mime and frequently music. They are an important medium of entertainment and instruction woven from the substance of human experience, and are very often realistic and down-to-earth.

The first African stories to reach western ears were written down only at the turn of the century when a number of missionaries, anthropologists and colonial officials arrived in Africa and made a concerted effort to record descriptions of the rituals and ceremonies they witnessed, and to transcribe as faithfully as possible tales told to them by old and young Africans before they had disappeared altogether. Some of these committed scholars wrote down what the elders told them about their gods, and man's understanding of his relationship with the gods, while others transcribed narrative myths, fables, poems, proverbs, riddles and even magic spells.

No real unified mythology exists in Africa, however. The migration of its peoples, the political fragmentation, and the sheer size of the continent have resulted in a huge diversity of lifestyles and traditions. Literally thousands of completely different languages are spoken, 2,000 in West Africa alone between the Senegal River and the headwaters of the Congo River. A complete collection of all myths of the African peoples would fill countless volumes, even if we were to ignore the fact that the collection is being added to all the time by modern-day enthusiasts.

To give a useful summary of the main characteristics of African mythology is therefore an extremely difficult task but, broadly speaking, a number of beliefs, ideas and themes are shared by African peoples, embellished by a creative spirit unique to a tribe, village or region. Nearly every tribe has its own set of cosmological myths – tales which attempt to explore the origin of the universe, the unseen forces of nature, the existence of God or a supreme being, the creation of mankind and the coming of mortality. Other stories, detailing the outrageous adventures and anti-social behaviour of one or another trickster figure are also common to nearly every tribe. Moral stories abound and animal fables, in particular, are some of the most popular of all African tales.

This book is divided into three chapters containing only a cross-section of African tales. It is intended to provide an introduction to African mythology and is in no way a comprehensive study of its subject. A selection of creation stories, animal fables and stories which amuse and teach, has been made with the aim of providing as interesting and entertaining an overview as possible.

Opposite: North Africa stretches from Morocco to Egypt, and down through the Nile valley to Ethiopia. This fertile region cradles a distinctly Mediterranean culture.

AUTHOR'S NOTE

It has been impossible to represent every region of southern Africa in a volume of this size, and the author has concentrated instead on presenting some of the most popular and well-known tales, many of which originate in west Africa, an area with the greatest concentration of different peoples, offering a particularly colourful mythological tradition.

MYTHS OF CREATION, DEATH AND THE AFTERLIFE

ost African peoples recognize some sort of all-powerful, omniscient god, but the sheer size of the African continent has not allowed a uniform system of beliefs to develop. Innumerable myths on the origin and evolution of the universe exist as a result. The Fon of Dahomey speak of a supreme God, Mawu-Lisa, the 'twins' from whom all the gods and demigods are descended. The Zulu of South Africa call their deity uKqili, the wise one, and believe he raised mankind out of 'beds of grass'. The Hottentots refer to their god as Utixo, a benevolent deity who inhabits the sky and speaks with the voice of thunder.

The creation myth retold at the beginning of this chapter comes from the Yoruba tribe in west Africa, whose pantheon alone contains over 1,700 deities. The most important Yoruban gods feature in the stories. Olorun, the supreme being, is capable of seeing both 'the inside and the outside of man', while the other gods are depicted as sensitive to human problems and particularly receptive to human prayers.

Again, nearly every tribe has its own story on the creation of mankind, the origin of death and darkness, and its own unique descriptions of the Otherworld. Only a selection of these tales is retold here, chosen from among the Krachi, Kikuyu and Kono peoples of Africa.

Creation Myth: The Creation of the Universe

(From the Yoruba people, west Africa)

BEFORE THE UNIVERSE WAS CREATED, there existed only a vast expanse of sky above and an endless stretch of water and uninhabited marshland below. Olorun, the wisest of the gods, was supreme ruler of the sky, while Olokun, the most powerful goddess, ruled the seas and marshes. Both kingdoms were quite separate at that time and there was never any conflict between the two deities. Olorun was more than satisfied with his domain in the sky and hardly noticed what took place below him. Olokun was content with the kingdom she occupied, even though it contained neither living creatures nor vegetation of any kind.

But the young god Obatala was not entirely satisfied with this state of affairs, and one day, as he looked down from the sky upon the dull, grey terrain ruled by Olokun, he thought to himself:

'The kingdom below is a pitiful, barren place. Something must be done to improve its murky appearance. Now if only there were mountains and forests to brighten it up, it would make a perfect home for all sorts of living creatures.'

Obatala decided that he must visit Olorun, who was always prepared to listen to him.

'It is a good scheme, but also a very ambitious one,' Olorun said to Obatala. 'I have no doubt that the hills and valleys you describe would be far better than grey ocean, but who will create this new world, and how will they go about it?'

'If you will give me your blessing,' Obatala replied, 'I myself will undertake to do this work.'

'Then it is settled,' said Olorun. 'I cannot help you myself, but I will arrange for you to visit my son Orunmila. He will be able to guide you.'

Next day, Obatala called upon Orunmila, the eldest son of Olorun, who had been given the power to read the future and to understand the secret of existence. Orunmila produced his divining tray, and when he had placed sixteen palm nuts on it, he shook the tray and cast its contents high into the air. As the nuts dropped to the ground, he read their meaning aloud:

'First, Obatala,' he announced, 'you must find a chain of gold long enough for you to climb down from the sky to the watery wastes below. Then, as you descend, take with you a snail shell filled with sand, a white hen, a black cat and a palm nut. This is how you should begin your quest.'

Obatala listened attentively to his friend's advice and immediately set off to find a goldsmith who would make him the chain he needed to descend from the sky to the surface of the water below.

'I would be happy to make you the chain you ask for,' said the goldsmith, 'provided you can give me all the gold I need. But I doubt that you will find enough here for me to complete my task.'

Obatala would not be dissuaded, however, and having instructed the goldsmith to go ahead with his work, he approached the other sky gods and one by one explained to them his purpose, requesting that they contribute whatever gold they possessed. The response was generous. Some of the gods gave gold dust, others gave rings, bracelets or pendants, and before long a huge, glittering mound had been collected. The goldsmith examined all the gold that was brought before him, but still he complained that there was not enough.

'It is the best I can do,' Obatala told him. 'I have asked all of the other gods to help out and there is no more gold left in the sky. Make the chain as long as you possibly can and fix a hook to one end. Even if it fails to reach the water below, I am determined to climb down on it.'

The goldsmith worked hard to complete the chain and when it was finished, the hook was fastened to the edge of the sky and the chain lowered far below. Orunmila appeared and handed Obatala a bag containing the sand-filled snail's shell, the white hen, the black cat and the palm nut, and as soon as he had slung it over his shoulder, the young god began climbing down the golden chain, lower and lower until he saw that he was leaving the world of light and entering a world of twilight.

Before long, Obatala could feel the damp mists rising up from the surface of the water, but at the same time, he realized that he had just about reached the end of his golden chain.

'I cannot jump from here,' he thought. 'If I let go of the chain I will fall into the sea and almost certainly drown.'

And while he looked around him rather helplessly, he suddenly heard a familiar voice calling to him from up above.

'Make use of the sand I gave you,' Orunmila instructed him, 'toss it into the water below.'

Obatala obeyed, and after he had poured out the sand, he heard Orunmila calling to him a second time:

'Release the white hen,' Orunmila cried.

Obatala reached into his bag and pulled out the white hen,

dropping her on to the waters beneath where he had sprinkled the sand. As soon as she had landed, the hen began to scratch in the sand, scattering it in all directions. Wherever the grains fell, dry land instantly appeared. The larger heaps of sand became hills, while the smaller heaps became valleys.

Obatala let go of his chain and jumped on to the solid earth. As he walked he smiled with pleasure, for the land now extended a great many miles in all directions. But he was proudest of the spot where his feet had first landed, and decided to name this place Ife. Stooping to the ground, he began digging a hole, and buried his palm nut in the soil. Immediately, a palm tree sprang up from the earth, shedding its seeds as it stretched to its full height so that other trees soon shot up around it. Obatala felled some of these trees and built for himself a sturdy house thatched with palm leaves. And here, in this place, he settled down, separated from the other sky gods, with only his black cat for company.

Creation Myth: Obatala Creates Mankind

(From the Yoruba people, west Africa)

OBATALA LIVED QUITE CONTENTEDLY in his new home beneath the skies, quite forgetting that Olorun might wish to know how his plans were progressing. The supreme god soon grew impatient for news and ordered Agemo, the chameleon, to go down the golden chain to investigate. The chameleon descended and when he arrived at Ife, he knocked timidly on Obatala's door.

'Olorun has sent me here,' he said, 'to discover whether or not you have been successful in your quest.'

'Certainly I have,' replied Obatala, 'look around you and you will see the land I have created and the plants I have raised from the soil. Tell Olorun that it is now a far more pleasant kingdom than it was before, and that I would be more than willing to spend the rest of my time here, except that I am growing increasingly weary of the twilight and long to see brightness once more.'

Opposite: As the weeks turned to months, Obatala became unsettled once more and began to dream of spending time in the company of other beings who could move and speak.

Agemo returned home and reported to Olorun all that he had seen and heard. Olorun smiled, for it pleased him greatly that Obatala had achieved what he had set out to do. The young god, who was among his favourites, had earned a special reward, and so Olorun fashioned with his own hands a dazzling golden orb and tossed it into the sky.

'For you, Obatala, I have created the sun,' said Olorun, 'it will shed warmth and light on the new world you have brought to life below.'

Obatala very gladly received this gift, and as soon as he felt the first rays of the sun shining down on him, his restless spirit grew calmer. He remained quite satisfied for a time, but then, as the weeks turned to months, he became unsettled once more and began to dream of spending time in the company of other beings, not unlike himself, who could move and speak and with whom he could share his thoughts and feelings.

Obatala sat down and began to claw at the soil as he attempted to picture the little creatures who would keep him company. He found that the clay was soft and pliable, so he began to shape tiny figures in his own image. He laid the first of them in the sun to dry and worked on with great enthusiasm until he had produced several more.

He had been sitting for a long time in the hot sunshine before he realized how tired and thirsty he felt.

'What I need is some palm wine to revive me,' he thought to himself, and he stood up and headed off towards the nearest palm tree.

He placed his bowl underneath it and drew off the palm juice, leaving it to ferment in the heat until it had turned to wine. When the wine was ready, Obatala helped himself to a very long drink, and as he gulped down bowl after bowl of the refreshing liquid, he failed to realize that the wine was making him quite drunk.

Obatala had swallowed so much of the wine that his fingers grew clumsy, but he continued to work energetically, too drunk to notice that the clay figures he now produced were no longer perfectly formed. Some had crooked backs or crooked limbs, others had arms and legs of uneven length. Obatala was so pleased with himself he raised his head and called out jubilantly to the skies:

'I have created beings from the soil, but only you, Olorun, can breathe life into them. Grant me this request so that I will always have human beings to keep me company here in Ife.'

Olorun heard Obatala's plea and did not hesitate to breathe life into the clay figures, watching with interest as they rose up from the ground and began to obey the commands of their creator. Soon they had built wooden shelters for themselves next to the god's own house, creating the first Yoruba village in Ife where before only one solitary house had stood. Obatala was filled with admiration and pride, but now, as the effects of the palm wine started to wear off, he began to notice that some of the humans he had created were contorted and misshapen. The sight of the little creatures struggling as they went about their chores filled him with sadness and remorse.

'My drunkenness has caused these people to suffer,' he proclaimed solemnly, 'and I swear that I will never drink palm wine again. From this day forward, I will be the special protector of all humans who are born with deformities.'

Obatala remained faithful to his pledge and dedicated himself to the welfare of the human beings he had created, making sure that he always had a moment to spare for the lame and the blind. He saw to it that the people prospered and, before long, the Yoruba village of Ife had grown into an impressive city. Obatala also made certain that his people had all the tools they needed to clear and cultivate the land. He presented each man with a copper bush knife and a wooden hoe and taught them to grow millet, yams and a whole variety of other crops, ensuring that mankind had a plentiful supply of food for its survival.

Opposite:
Olorun then heard Obatala's plea and did not hesitate to breathe life into the clay figures, watching with interest as they rose up and began to obey their creator's commands.

Creation Myth: Olokun's Revenge

(From the Yoruba people, west Africa)

AFTER HE HAD LIVED among the human race for a long period of time, Obatala came to the decision that he had done all he could for his people. The day had arrived for him to retire, he believed, and so he climbed up the golden chain and returned to his home in the sky once more, promising to visit the earth as frequently as possible. The other gods never tired of hearing Obatala describe the kingdom he had created below. Many were so captivated by the image he presented of the newly created human beings, that they decided to depart from the sky and go down to live among them. And as they prepared to leave, Olorun took them aside and counselled them:

'Each of you shall have a special role while you are down there, and I ask that you never forget your duty to the human race. Always listen to the prayers of the people and offer help when they are in need.'

One deity, however, was not at all pleased with Obatala's work or the praise he had received from Olorun. The goddess Olokun, ruler of the sea, watched with increasing fury as, one by one, the other gods arrived in her domain and began dividing up the land amongst themselves.

'Obatala has never once consulted me about any of this,' she announced angrily, 'but he shall pay for the insult to my honour.'

The goddess commanded the great waves of her ocean to rise up, for it was her intention to destroy the land Obatala had created and replace it with water once more. The terrible flood began, and soon the fields were completely submerged. Crops were destroyed and thousands of people were swept away by the roaring tide.

Those who survived the deluge fled to the hills and called to Obatala for help, but he could not hear them from his home high above in the sky.

In desperation, the people turned to Eshu, one of the gods recently descended to earth.

'Please return to the sky,' they begged, 'and tell the great gods of the flood that threatens to destroy everything.'

'First you must show that you revere the gods,' replied Eshu. 'You must offer up a sacrifice and pray hard that you will be saved.'

The people went away and returned with a goat which they sacrificed as food for Obatala. But still Eshu refused to carry the message.

'You ask me to perform this great service,' he told them, 'and yet

Opposite:
Among Olorun's most trusted envoys was the chameleon, Agemo. It was this creature the god turned to for help while in conflict with Olokun, ruler of the seas.

you do not offer to reward me. If I am to be your messenger, I too deserve a gift.'

The people offered up more sacrifices to Eshu and only when he was content that they had shown him appropriate respect did he begin to climb the golden chain back to the sky to deliver his message.

Obatala was deeply upset by the news and extremely anxious for the safety of his people, for he was uncertain how best to deal with so powerful a goddess as Olokun. Once more, he approached Orunmila and asked for advice. Orunmila consulted his divining nuts, and at last he said to Obatala:

'Rest here in the sky while I descend below. I will use my gifts to turn back the water and make the land rise again.'

Orunmila went down and, using his special powers, brought the waves under control so that the marshes began to dry up and land became visible again. But although the people greeted the god as their saviour and pleaded with him to act as their protector, Orunmila confessed that he had no desire to remain among them. Before he departed, however, he passed on a great many of his gifts to the people, teaching them how to divine the future and to control the unseen forces of nature. What he taught the people was never lost and it was passed on like a precious heirloom from one generation to another.

Creation Myth: Agemo Outwits Olokun

(From the Yoruba people, west Africa)

BUT EVEN AFTER ORUNMILA had returned to his home in the sky, all was not yet settled between Olokun and the other sky gods. More embittered than ever before by her defeat, Olokun began to consider ways in which she might humiliate Olorun, the god who had allowed Obatala to usurp her kingdom.

Now the goddess was a highly skilled weaver, but she was also expert in dyeing the cloths she had woven. And knowing that no other sky god possessed greater knowledge of clothmaking, she sent a message to Olorun challenging him to a weaving contest. Olorun received her message rather worriedly and said to himself:

'Olokun knows far more about making cloth that I will ever know, but I cannot allow her to think that she is superior to me in anything. Somehow I must appear to meet her challenge and yet avoid taking part in the contest. But how can I possibly do this?'

He pondered the problem a very long time until, at last, he was struck by a worthwhile thought. Smiling broadly, he summoned Agemo, the chameleon, to his side, and instructed him to carry an important message to Olokun.

Agemo climbed down the golden chain and went in search of Olokun's dwelling.

'The ruler of the sky, Olorun, greets you,' he announced. 'He says that if your cloth is as magnificent as you say it is, then the ruler of the sky will be happy to compete with you in the contest you have suggested. But he thinks it only fair to see some of your cloth in advance, and has asked me to examine it on his behalf so that I may report to him on its quality.'

Olokun was happy to accommodate Olorun's request. She retired to a backroom and having put on a skirt of radiant green cloth, she stood confidently before the chameleon. But as the chameleon looked at the garment, his skin began to change colour until it was exactly the same brilliant shade as the skirt. Next Olokun put on an orange-hued cloth. But again, to her astonishment, the chameleon turned a beautiful shade of bright orange. One by one, the goddess put on skirts of various bright colours, but on each occasion the chameleon perfectly matched the colour of her robe. Finally the goddess thought to herself:

'This person is only a messenger, and if Olorun's servants can reproduce the exact colours of my very finest cloth, what hope

Opposite:
Using his special powers, Orunmila brought the waves under control so that the marshes began to dry up and the land became visible again.

will I have in a contest against the supreme god himself?'

The goddess conceded defeat and spoke earnestly to the chameleon:

'Tell your master that the ruler of the seas sends her greetings to the ruler of the sky. Say to him that I acknowledge his supremacy in weaving and in all other things as well.'

And so it came to pass that Olorun and Olokun resumed their friendship and that peace was restored to the whole of the universe once more.

The Gods Descend from the Sky
(From the Dahomean people, west Africa)

NANA BALUKU, the mother of all creation, fell pregnant before she finally retired from the universe. Her offspring was androgynous, a being with one body and two faces. The face that resembled a woman was called Mawu and her eyes were the moon. She took control of the night and all territories to the west. The male face was called Lisa and his eyes were the sun. Lisa controlled the east and took charge of the daylight.

At the beginning of the present world, Mawu-Lisa was the only being in existence, but eventually the moon was eclipsed by the sun and many children were conceived. The first fruits of the union were a pair of twins, a male called Da Zodji and a female called Nyohwè Ananu. Another child followed shortly afterwards, a male and female form joined in one body, and this child was named Sogbo. The third birth again produced twins, a male, Agbè, and a female, Naètè. The fourth and fifth children were both male and were named Agè and Gu. Gu's torso was made of stone and a giant sword protruded from the hole in his neck where his head would otherwise have been. The sixth offspring was not made of flesh and blood. He was given the name Djo, meaning air, or atmosphere. Finally, the seventh child born was named Legba, and because he was the youngest, he became Mawu-Lisa's particular favourite.

Opposite:
Agè was ordered to live in the bush as a hunter where he could take control of all the birds and beasts of the earth.

When these children had grown to adulthood and the appropriate time had arrived to divide up the kingdoms of the universe among them, Mawu-Lisa gathered them together. To their first-born, the twins Da Zodji and Nyohwè Ananu, the parents gave the earth below and sent them, laden with heavenly riches, down from the sky to

inhabit their new home. To Sogbo, who was both man and woman, they gave the sky, commanding him to rule over thunder and lightning. The twins Agbè and Naètè were sent to take command of the waters and the creatures of the deep, while Agè was ordered to live in the bush as a hunter where he could take control of all the birds and beasts of the earth.

To Gu, whom Mawu-Lisa considered their strength, they gave the forests and vast stretches of fertile soil, supplying him also with the tools and weapons mankind would need to cultivate the land. Mawu-Lisa ordered Djo to occupy the space between the earth and the sky and entrusted him with the life-span of human beings. It was also Djo's role to clothe the other sky gods, making them invisible to man.

To each of their offspring, Mawu-Lisa then gave a special language. These are the languages still spoken by the priests and mediums of the gods in their songs and oracles. To Da Zodji and Nyohwè Ananu, Mawu-Lisa gave the language of the earth and took from them all memory of the sky language. They gave to Sogbo, Agbè and Naètè, Agè and Gu the languages they would speak. But to Djo, they gave the language of men.

Then Mawu-Lisa said to Legba: 'Because you are my youngest child, I will keep you with me always. Your work will be to visit all the kingdoms ruled over by your brothers and sisters and report to me on their progress.'

And that is why Legba knows all the languages of his siblings, and he alone knows the language of Mawu-Lisa. You will find Legba everywhere, because all beings, human and gods, must first approach Legba before Mawu-Lisa, the supreme deity, will answer their prayers.

God Abandons the Earth

(From Ghana, west Africa)

IN THE BEGINNING, God was very proud of the human beings he had created and wanted to live as close as possible to them. So he made certain that the sky was low enough for the people to touch and built for himself a home directly above their heads. God was so near that everyone on earth became familiar with his face and every day he would stop to make conversation with the people, offering a helping hand if they were ever in trouble.

This arrangement worked very well at first, but soon God

Opposite:
To Gu, whom Mawu-Lisa considered their strength, they gave the forests and fertile soil, supplying him also with the tools mankind would need.

observed that the people had started to take advantage of his closeness. Children began to wipe their greasy hands on the sky when they had finished their meals and often, if a woman was in search of an extra ingredient for dinner, she would simply reach up, tear a piece off the sky and add it to her cooking pot. God remained tolerant through all of this, but he knew his patience would not last forever and hoped that his people would not test its limit much further.

Then one afternoon, just as he had lain down to rest, a group of women gathered underneath the sky to pound the corn they had harvested. One old woman among them had a particularly large wooden bowl and a very long pestle, and as she thumped down on the grains, she knocked violently against the sky. God arose indignantly from his bed and descended below, but as he approached the woman to chastise her, she suddenly jerked back her arm and hit him in the eye with her very long pestle.

God gave a great shout, his voice booming like thunder through the air, and as he shouted, he raised his powerful arms above his head and pushed upwards against the sky with all his strength, flinging it far into the distance.

As soon as they realized that the earth and the sky were separated, the people became angry with the old woman who had injured God and pestered her day and night to bring him back to them. The woman went away and although she was not very clever, she thought long and hard about the problem until she believed she had found the solution. Returning to her village, she ordered her children to collect all the wooden mortars that they could find. These she piled one on top of the other until they had almost bridged the gap between the earth and the heavens. Only one more mortar was needed to complete the job, but although her children searched high and low, they could not find the missing object. In desperation, the old woman told them to remove the lowest mortar from the bottom of the pile and place it on the top. But as soon as they did this, all the mortars came crashing down, killing the old woman, her children and the crowd who had gathered to admire the towering structure.

Opposite: God raised his powerful arms above his head and pushed upwards against the sky with all his strength, flinging it far into the distance.

Ever since that day, God has remained in the heavens where mankind can no longer approach him as easily as before. There are some, however, who say they have caught a glimpse of him and others who offer up sacrifices calling for his forgiveness and asking him to make his home among them once more.

The Coming of Darkness

(From the Kono people, Sierra Leone)

WHEN GOD FIRST MADE THE WORLD, there was never any darkness or cold. The sun always shone brightly during the day, and at night, the moon bathed the earth in a softer light, ensuring that everything could still be seen quite clearly.

But one day God sent for the Bat and handed him a mysterious parcel to take to the moon. He told the Bat it contained darkness, but as he did not have the time to explain precisely what darkness was, the Bat went on his way without fully realizing the importance of his mission.

He flew at a leisurely pace with the parcel strapped on his back until he began to feel rather tired and hungry. He was in no great hurry he decided, and so he put down his load by the roadside and wandered off in search of something to eat.

But while he was away, a group of mischievous animals approached the spot where he had paused to rest and, seeing the parcel, began to open it, thinking there might be something of value inside of it. The Bat returned just as they were untying the last piece of string and rushed forward to stop them. But too late! The darkness forced its way through the opening and rose up into the sky before anyone had a chance to catch it.

Quickly the Bat gave chase, flying about everywhere, trying to grab hold of the darkness and return it to the parcel before God discovered what had happened. But the harder he tried, the more the darkness eluded him, so that eventually he fell into an exhausted sleep lasting several hours.

When the Bat awoke, he found himself in a strange twilight world and once again, he began chasing about in every direction, hoping he would succeed where he had failed before.

But the Bat has never managed to catch the darkness, although you will see him every evening just after the sun has set, trying to trap it and deliver it safely to the moon as God first commanded him.

The Sun and the Moon

(From the Krachi people, west Africa)

THE SUN AND THE MOON fell in love and decided to marry. For a time they were very happy together and produced many children whom they christened 'stars'. But it was not long before the moon grew weary of her husband and decided to take a lover, refusing to conceal the fact that she greatly enjoyed the variety.

Of course, the sun soon came to hear of his wife's brazen infidelity and the news made him extremely unhappy. He attempted to reason with the moon, but when he saw that his efforts were entirely fruitless, he decided to drive his wife out of his house. Some of the children sided with their mother, while others supported their father. But the sun was never too hard on his wife, in spite of their differences, and saw to it that their possessions were equally divided up.

The moon was always too proud to accept her husband's kindness, however, and even to this day, she continues to make a habit of trespassing on his lands, often taking her children with her and encouraging them to fight the siblings who remain behind with their father.

The constant battles between the star-children of the sun and the star-children of the moon produce great storms of thunder and lightning and it is only when she becomes bored of these confrontations that the moon sends her messenger, the rainbow, into the field, instructing him to wave a cloth of many colours as a signal for her children to retreat.

Sometimes the moon herself is caught by the sun attempting to steal crops from his fields. Whenever this happens, he chases after his estranged wife and if he catches her he begins to flog her or even tries to eat her.

So whenever a man sees an eclipse, he knows that things have come to blows once again between husband and wife up above. At this time, he must be certain to beat his drum and threaten the sun very loudly, for if he does not, the sun might finish the job, and we should certainly lose the moon forever.

How Death First Entered the World

(From the Krachi people, west Africa)

MANY YEARS AGO, a great famine spread throughout the land, and at that time, the eldest son of every household was sent out in search of food and instructed not to return until he had found something for the family to eat and drink.

There was a certain young man among the Krachi whose responsibility it was to provide for the family, and so he wandered off in search of food, moving deeper and deeper into the bush every day until he finally came to a spot he did not recognize. Just up ahead of him, he noticed a large form lying on the ground. He approached it cautiously, hoping that if the creature were dead, it might be a good source of food, but he had taken only a few steps forward when the mound began to stir, revealing that it was not an animal at all, but a ferocious-looking giant with flowing white hair stretched out for miles on the ground around him, all the way from Krachi to Salaga.

The giant opened one eye and shouted at the young man to explain his presence. The boy stood absolutely terrified, yet after some minutes, he managed to blurt out that he had never intended to disturb the giant's rest, but had come a great distance in search of food.

'I am Owuo,' said the giant, 'but people also call me Death. You, my friend, have caught me in a good mood and so I will give you some food and water if you will fetch and carry for me in return.'

The young man could scarcely believe his luck, and readily agreed to serve the giant in exchange for a few regular meals. Owuo arose and walked towards his cave where he began roasting some meat on a spit over the fire. Never before had the boy tasted such a fine meal, and after he had washed it down with a bowl of fresh water, he sat back and smiled, well pleased that he had made the acquaintance of the giant.

For a long time afterwards, the young man happily served Owuo, and every evening, in return for his work, he was presented with a plate of the most delicious meat for his supper.

Opposite: The eldest son of every household was sent out in search of food and instructed not to return until he had found something for the family to eat and drink.

But one day the boy awoke feeling terribly homesick and begged his master to allow him to visit his family, if only for a few days.

'You may visit your family for as long as you wish,' said the giant, 'on the condition that you bring another boy to replace you.'

So the young man returned to his village where he told his family

the whole story of his meeting with the giant. Eventually he managed to persuade his younger brother to go with him into the bush and here he handed him over to Owuo, promising that he would himself return before too long.

Several months had passed, and soon the young man grew hungry again and began to yearn for a taste of the meat the giant had cooked for him. Finally, he made up his mind to return to his master, and leaving his family behind, he returned to Owuo's hut and knocked boldly on the door.

The giant himself answered, and asked the young man what he wanted.

'I would like some more of the good meat you were once so generous to share with me,' said the boy, hoping the giant would remember his face.

'Very well,' replied Owuo, 'you can have as much of it as you want, but you will have to work hard for me, as you did before.'

The young man consented, and after he had eaten as much as he could, he went about his chores enthusiastically. The work lasted many weeks and every day the boy ate his fill of roasted meat. But to his surprise he never saw anything of his brother, and whenever he asked about him, the giant told him, rather aloofly, that the lad had simply gone away on business.

Once more, however, the young man grew homesick and asked Owuo for permission to visit his village. The giant agreed on condition that this time, he bring back a girl to carry out his duties while he was away. The young man hurried home and there he pleaded with his sister to go into the bush and keep the giant company for a few months. The girl agreed, and after she had waved goodbye to her brother, she entered the giant's cave quite merrily, accompanied by a slave companion her own age.

Only a short time had passed before the boy began to dream of the meat again, longing for even a small morsel of it. So he followed the familiar path through the bush until he found Owuo's cave. The giant did not seem particularly pleased to see him and grumbled loudly at the disturbance. But he pointed the way to a room at the back and told the boy to help himself to as much meat as he wanted.

The young man took up a juicy bone which he began to devour. But to his horror, he recognized it at once as his sister's thigh and as he looked more closely at all the rest of the meat, he was appalled to discover that he had been sitting there, happily chewing on the body of his sister and her slave girl.

As fast as his legs could carry him, he raced back to the village and immediately confessed to the elders what he had done and the awful things he had seen. At once, the alarm was sounded and all the people hurried out into the bush to investigate the giant's dwelling for themselves. But as they drew nearer, they became fearful of what he might do to them and scurried back to the village to consult among themselves what steps should be taken. Eventually, it was agreed to go to Salaga, where they knew the giant's long hair came to an end, and set it alight. The chief of the village carried the torch, and when they were certain that the giant's hair was burning well, they returned to the bush, hid themselves in the undergrowth, and awaited the giant's reaction.

Presently, Owuo began to sweat and toss about inside his cave. The closer the flames moved towards him, the more he thrashed about and grumbled until, at last, he rushed outside, his head on fire, and fell down screaming in agony.

The villagers approached him warily and only the young man had the courage to venture close enough to see whether the giant was still breathing. And as he bent over the huge form, he noticed a bundle of medicine concealed in the roots of Owuo's hair. Quickly he seized it and called to the others to come and see what he had found.

The chief of the village examined the bundle, but no one could say what power the peculiar medicine might have. Then one old man among the crowd suggested that no harm could be done if they took some of the medicine and sprinkled it on the bones and meat in the giant's hut. This was done, and to the delight of everyone gathered, the slave girl, her mistress and the boy's brother returned to life at once.

A small quantity of the medicine-dust remained, but when the young man proposed that he should put it on the giant and restore him to life, there was a great uproar among the people. Yet the boy insisted that he should help the giant who had once helped him, and so the chief, by way of compromise, allowed him to sprinkle the left-over dust into the eye of the dead giant.

The young man had no sooner done this when the giant's eye opened wide, causing the people to flee in great terror.

But it is from this eye that death comes. For every time that Owuo shuts that eye, a man dies, and unfortunately for mankind, he is forever blinking and winking, trying to clear the dust from his eye.

Wanjiru, Sacrificed by Her Family

(From the Kikuyu people, Kenya)

THE SUN BEAT DOWN mercilessly and there was no sign of any rain. This happened one year, and it happened again a second year, and even a third year, so that the crops died and the men, women and children found themselves close to starvation. Finally, the elders of the village called all the people together, and they assembled on the scorched grass at the foot of the hill where they had sung and danced in happier times.

Sick and weary of their miserable plight, they turned to each other and asked helplessly:

'Why is it that the rains do not come?'

Not one among them could find an answer, and so they went to the house of the witch-doctor and put to him the same question:

'Tell us why there is no rain,' they wept. 'Our crops have failed for a third season and we shall soon die of hunger if things do not change.'

The witch-doctor took hold of his gourd, shook it hard, and poured its contents on the ground. After he had done this three times, he spoke gravely:

'There is a young maiden called Wanjiru living among you. If you want the rain to fall, she must be bought by the people of the village. In two days time you should all return to this place, and every one of you, from the eldest to the youngest, must bring with him a goat for the purchase of the maiden.'

And so, on the appointed day, the people gathered together again, each one of them leading a goat to the foot of the hill where the witch-doctor waited to receive them. He ordered the crowd to form a circle and called for Wanjiru to come forward and stand in the middle with her relations to one side of her.

One by one, the people began to move towards Wanjiru's family, leading the goats in payment, and as they approached, the feet of the young girl began to sink into the ground. In an instant, she had sunk up to her knees and she screamed in terror as the soil tugged at her limbs, pulling her closer towards the earth.

Her father and mother saw what was happening and they, too, cried out in fear:

'Our daughter is lost! Our daughter is lost! We must do something to save her.'

Opposite:
The people began to move towards Wanjiru's family, leading the goats; as they approached, the feet of the young girl sank into the ground.

But the villagers continued to close in around them, each of them handing over their goat until Wanjiru sank deeper to her waist.

'I am lost!' the girl called out, 'but much rain will come.'

She sank to her breast, and as she did so, heavy black clouds began to gather overhead. She sank even lower, up to her neck, and now the rain started to fall from above in huge drops.

Again, Wanjiru's family attempted to move forward to save her, but yet more people came towards them, pressing them to take goats in payment, and so they stood still, watching as the girl wailed:

'My people have forsaken me! I am undone.'

Soon she had vanished from sight. The earth closed over her, the rain poured down in a great deluge and the villagers ran to their huts for shelter without pausing to look back.

Now there was a particular young warrior of fearless reputation among the people, who had been in love with Wanjiru ever since childhood. Several weeks had passed since her disappearance, but still he could not reconcile himself to her loss and repeated continually to himself:

'Wanjiru is gone from me and her own people have done this thing to her. But I will find her. I will go to the same place and bring her back.'

Taking up his shield and his spear, the young warrior departed his home in search of the girl he loved. For almost a year, he roamed the countryside, but still he could find no trace of her. Weary and dejected, he returned home to the village and stood on the spot where Wanjiru had vanished, allowing his tears to flow freely for the first time.

Suddenly, his feet began to sink into the soil and he sank lower and lower until the ground closed over him and he found himself standing in the middle of a long, winding road beneath the earth's surface. He did not hesitate to follow this road, and after a time, he spotted a figure up ahead of him. He ran towards the figure and saw that it was Wanjiru, even though she was scarcely recognizable in her filthy, tattered clothing.

'You were sacrificed to bring the rain,' he spoke tenderly to her, 'but now that the rain has come, I shall take you back where you belong.'

Opposite:
There was a particular young warrior of fearless reputation among the people, who had been in love with Wanjiru ever since childhood.

And he lifted Wanjiru carefully onto his back and carried her, as if she were his own beloved child, along the road he had come by, until they rose together to the open air and their feet touched the ground once more.

'You shall not return to the house of your people,' the warrior told Wanjiru, 'they have treated you shamefully. I will look after you instead.'

So they waited until nightfall, and under cover of darkness, the young warrior took Wanjiru to his mother's house, instructing the old woman to tell no one that the girl had returned.

The months passed by, and Wanjiru lived happily with mother and son. Every day a goat was slaughtered and the meat served to her. The old woman made clothes from the skins and hung beads in the girl's hair so that soon she had regained the healthy glow she once had.

Harvest time was now fast approaching, and a great feast was to be held among the people of the village. The young warrior was one of the first to arrive but Wanjiru waited until the rest of the guests had assembled before she came out of the house to join the festivities. At first, she was not recognized by anyone, but after a time, one of her brothers approached her and cried out:

'Surely that is Wanjiru, the sister we lost when the rains came.'

The girl hung her head and gave no answer.

'You sold Wanjiru shamefully,' the young warrior intervened, 'you do not deserve to have her back.'

And he beat off her relatives and took Wanjiru back to his mother's house.

But the next day, her family knocked on his door asking to see the young girl. The warrior refused them once more, but still they came, again and again, until, on the fourth day, the young man relented and said to himself:

'Those are real tears her family shed. Surely now they have proven that they care.'

So he invited her father and her mother and her brothers into his home and sat down to fix the bride-price for Wanjiru. And when he had paid it, the young warrior married Wanjiru who had returned to him from the land of shadows beneath the earth.

✳   ✳   ✳

ANIMAL FABLES

FABLE IS A SHORT MORAL STORY, and the African storyteller has shown a particular fondness for this sort of tale in which the actions and escapades of the characters are described not merely for our entertainment, but also for us to reflect on and from which to learn lessons.

Many African fables revolve entirely around animals, and the stories which follow are a selection of some of the most well-known. In all of the fables, animals have the ability to speak and they generally behave like humans. Some, like the chameleon in the last story, even marry human beings.

Two of the most outstanding characters of the animal fables are the spider and the tortoise. The first three stories of this section centre on the adventures of the shrewd and designing spider Anansi, who usually manages to outwit all of his opponents, yet whose behaviour is not always intended to reflect the correct moral course. The stories chosen originate in west Africa, although similar fables are told throughout the whole of the African continent.

Equally shrewd and clever, despite his slow-moving body and wrinkled skin, is the tortoise who, again and again, triumphs over his adversaries. In the four tales which follow, it is his uncanny wisdom that shines through, ensuring that he is never defeated, even by those who are much larger and stronger.

Tales of Anansi, the Spider Trickster

How Anansi Became a Spider

(From the Dagomba people, west Africa)

A VERY LONG TIME AGO, there lived a king who had amongst his possessions a very magnificent ram, larger and taller than any other specimen in the entire country. The ram was more precious to him than anything else he owned and he made it quite clear to his subjects that the animal must be allowed to roam wherever it chose, and be allowed to eat as much food as it desired, even if the people themselves were forced to go hungry. If anyone should ever hit or injure the king's ram, that man should certainly die.

Every citizen of the kingdom obeyed the king's orders without a great deal of complaint, but there was one among them, a wealthy farmer named Anansi, who was particularly proud of the crops he raised. Everyone suspected that he would not tolerate a visit from the king's ram and they prayed amongst themselves that such an event might never happen.

One day, however, when the rains had begun to fall, and his crops were already as tall as his waist, Anansi went out to make a final inspection of his fields. He was very pleased with what he saw and was just about to return to his farmhouse when he noticed in the distance an area of land where the corn had been trampled underfoot and the young shoots eaten away. There in the middle of the field, still munching away quite happily, stood the king's ram. Anansi was so furious he hurled a large pebble at the animal intending only to frighten him away. But the stone hit the ram right between the eyes and before he had quite realized what he had done, the animal lay dead at his feet.

Anansi did not know what he should do. Like everybody else in the village, he was only too familiar with the king's orders and knew he would face certain death if his crime was discovered. He leaned back against a shea-butter tree wondering how to resolve the dreadful mess. Suddenly a nut fell on his head from one of the branches above. Anansi picked it up and ate it. He liked the taste of it very much and so he shook the tree until several more nuts fell to the ground. Then the most fantastic idea entered his head. He picked up the nuts and put them in his pocket. He quickly lifted the ram and climbed the tree with him. As soon as he had tied the animal to a strong bough he descended once more and headed off towards the house of his friend, Kusumbuli, the spider.

Opposite: Anansi, the spider trickster, whose behaviour is not always intended to reflect the correct moral course, still usually manages to outwit all of his opponents.

Anansi found his friend at home and the two sat down and began to chat. After a few moments, Anansi took one of the shea-nuts from his pocket and handed it to his friend.

'This nut has an excellent flavour,' said Kusumbuli, as he sat chomping on the ripe flesh, 'tell me, where did you come across such a fine crop?'

Anansi promised to show the spider the exact spot and led him to the tree where the nuts were growing in large clusters.

'You'll have to shake quite hard to loosen them,' Anansi advised Kusumbuli, 'don't be afraid, the trunk is a strong one.'

So the spider began shaking the tree violently and as he did so, the dead ram fell to the ground.

'Oh, my friend,' cried Anansi at once, 'what have you done? Look, the king's ram is lying at your feet and you have killed him.'

Kusumbuli turned pale as a wave of panic swept over him.

'There is only one thing you can do now,' Anansi urged the spider, 'go and unburden your conscience at once. Tell the king precisely what has happened and with any luck he will understand that the whole affair was a most unfortunate accident.'

Kusumbuli thought that this was good advice, so he picked up the dead ram and set off to confess his crime, hoping the king would be in a good mood.

The road towards the king's palace brought him past his own home and the spider went indoors to bid a sad farewell to his wife and children, believing that he might never set eyes on them again. Anansi stood at the entrance while Kusumbuli went into the back room and told his wife everything that had happened. She listened attentively to what he said and immediately saw that there was some trick involved.

'I have never seen a ram climb a tree before, Kusumbuli,' she said to him. 'Use your head. Anansi has something to do with this and you are taking the blame for him. Hear me now and do exactly as I say.'

So she advised her husband that he must leave Anansi behind and pretend to go alone in search of the king. After he had gone some distance, she told him, he was to rest and then return home and announce that all had turned out well in the end. The spider agreed to do this and asked Anansi if he would be so good as to look after his wife and children. His friend promised to watch over them faithfully and the spider set off on his travels winking at his wife as he moved away.

Opposite: Many African fables revolve around animals. In all of the fables, animals have the ability to speak and they generally behave like humans.

Several hours later, Kusumbuli returned to his home, smiling from ear to ear as he embraced his family.

'Come and celebrate with us, Anansi,' he cried excitedly, 'I have been to see the king and he was not at all angry with me. In fact, he said he had no use for a dead ram and insisted that I help myself to as much of the meat as I wanted.'

At this, Anansi became enraged and shouted out:

'What! You have been given all that meat when it was I who took the trouble to kill that ram. I should have been given my fair share, you deserved none of it.'

Kusumbuli and his wife now leaped upon Anansi and bound his hands and legs. Then they dragged him to the king's palace and reported to their ruler the whole unpleasant affair.

Anansi squirmed on the floor and begged for the king's mercy. But the king could not control his fury and he raised his foot to kick Anansi as he lay on the ground. The king kicked so hard that Anansi broke into a thousand pieces that scattered themselves all over the room.

And that is how Anansi came to be such a small spider. And that is why you will find him in every corner of the house, awaiting the day when someone will put all the pieces together again.

Anansi Obtains the Sky-God's Stories

(From the Ashanti people, west Africa)

KWAKU ANANSI HAD ONE GREAT WISH. He longed to be the owner of all the stories known in the world, but these were kept by the Sky-God, Nyame[1], in a safe hiding-place high above the clouds.

One day, Anansi decided to pay the Sky-God a visit to see if he could persuade Nyame to sell him the stories.

'I am flattered you have come so far, little creature,' the Sky-God told Anansi, 'but many rich and powerful men have preceded you and none has been able to purchase what they came here for. I am willing to part with my stories, but the price is very high. What makes you think that you can succeed where they have all failed?'

'I feel sure I will be able to buy them,' answered Anansi bravely, 'if you will only tell me what the price is.'

'You are very determined, I see,' replied Nyame, 'but I must warn you that the price is no ordinary one. Listen carefully now to what I demand of you.

'First of all, you must capture Onini, the wise old python, and present him to me. When you have done this, you must go in search of the Mmoboro, the largest nest of hornets in the forest, and bring them here also. Finally, look for Osebo, the fastest of all leopards and set a suitable trap for him. Bring him to me either dead or alive.

'When you have delivered me these three things, all the stories of the world will be handed over to you.'

'I shall bring you everything you ask for,' Anansi declared firmly, and he hastened towards his home where he began making plans for the tasks ahead.

That afternoon, he sat down with his wife, Aso, and told her all about his visit to the Sky-God.

'How will I go about trapping the great python, Onini?' he asked her.

His wife, who was a very clever woman, instructed her husband to make a special trip to the centre of the woods:

'Go and cut yourself a long bamboo pole,' she ordered him, 'and gather some strong creeper-vines as well. As soon as you have done this, return here to me and I will tell you what to do with these things.'

Anansi gathered these objects as his wife had commanded and after they had spent some hours consulting further, he set off enthusiastically towards the house of Onini.

As he approached, he suddenly began arguing with himself in a loud and angry voice:

'My wife is a stupid woman,' he pronounced, 'she says it is longer and stronger. I say it is shorter and weaker. She has no respect. I have a great deal. She is stupid. I am right.'

'What's all this about?' asked the python, suddenly appearing at the door of his hut. 'Why are you having this angry conversation with yourself?'

'Oh! Please ignore me,' answered the spider. 'It's just that my wife has put me in such a bad mood. For she says this bamboo pole is longer and stronger than you are, and I say she is a liar.'

'There is no need for the two of you to argue so bitterly on my account,' replied the python, 'bring that pole over here and we will soon find out who is right.'

So Anansi laid the bamboo pole on the earth and the python stretched himself out alongside it.

'I'm still not certain about this,' said Anansi after a few moments. 'When you stretch at one end, you appear to shrink at the other end. Perhaps if I tied you to the pole I would have a clearer idea of your size.'

'Very well,' answered the python, 'just so long as we can sort this out properly.'

Anansi then took the creeper-vine and wrapped it round and round the length of the python's body until the great creature was unable to move.

'Onini,' said Anansi, 'it appears my wife was right. You are shorter and weaker than this pole and more foolish into the bargain. Now you are my prisoner and I must take you to the Sky-God, as I have promised.'

The great python lowered his head in defeat as Anansi tugged on the pole, dragging him along towards the home of Nyame.

'You have done well, spider,' said the god, 'but remember, there are two more, equally difficult quests ahead. You have much to accomplish yet, and it would not be wise to delay here any longer.'

So Anansi returned home once more and sat down to discuss the next task with his wife.

'There are still hornets to catch,' he told her, 'and I cannot think of a way to capture an entire swarm all at once.'

'Look for a gourd,' his wife suggested, 'and after you have filled it with water, go out in search of the hornets.'

Anansi found a suitable gourd and filled it to the brim. Fortunately, he knew exactly the tree where the hornets had built their nest. But before he approached too close, he poured some of the water from the gourd over himself so that his clothes were dripping wet. Then, he began sprinkling the nest with the remaining water while shouting out to the hornets:

'Why do you remain in such a flimsy shelter Mmoboro, when the great rains have already begun? You will soon be swept away, you foolish people. Here, take cover in this dry gourd of mine and it will protect you from the storms.'

Opposite:
'I shall bring you everything you ask for,' Anansi told the Sky-God and he hastened towards his home where he began making plans for the tasks ahead.

The hornets thanked the spider for this most timely warning and disappeared one by one into the gourd. As soon as the last of them had entered, Anansi plugged the mouth of the vessel with some grass and chuckled to himself:

'Fools! I have outwitted you as well. Now you can join Onini, the

python. I'm certain Nyame will be very pleased to see you.'

Anansi was delighted with himself. It had not escaped his notice that even the Sky-God appeared rather astonished by his success and it filled him with great excitement to think that very soon he would own all the stories of the world.

Only Osebo, the leopard, stood between the spider and his great wish, but Anansi was confident that with the help of his wife he could easily ensnare the creature as he had done all the others.

'You must go and look for the leopard's tracks,' his wife told him, 'and then dig a hole where you know he is certain to walk.'

Anansi went away and dug a very deep pit in the earth, covering it with branches and leaves so that it was well-hidden from the naked eye. Night-time closed in around him and soon afterwards, Osebo came prowling as usual and fell right into the deep hole, snarling furiously as he hit the bottom.

At dawn on the following morning, Anansi approached the giant pit and called to the leopard:

'What has happened here? Have you been drinking, leopard? How on earth will you manage to escape from this great hole?'

'I have fallen into a silly man-trap,' said the leopard impatiently. 'Help me out at once. I am almost starving to death in this wretched place.'

'And if I help you out, how can I be sure you won't eat me?' asked Anansi. 'You say you are very hungry, after all.'

'I wouldn't do a thing like that,' Osebo reassured him. 'I beg you, just this once, to trust me. Nothing bad will happen to you, I promise.'

Anansi hurried away from the opening of the pit and soon returned with a long, thick rope. Glancing around him, he spotted a tall green tree and bent it towards the ground, securing it with a length of the rope so that the top branches hung over the pit. Then he tied another piece of rope to these branches, dropping the loose end into the pit for the leopard to tie to his tail.

'As soon as you have tied a large knot, let me know and I will haul you up,' shouted Anansi.

Osebo obeyed the spider's every word, and as soon as he gave the signal that he was ready, Anansi cut the rope pinning the tree to the ground. It sprung upright at once, pulling the leopard out of the hole in one swift motion. Osebo hung upside down, wriggling and twisting helplessly, trying with every ounce of his strength to loosen his tail from the rope. But Anansi was not about to take any chances and he plunged his knife deep into the leopard's chest, killing him instantly. Then he lifted the leopard's body from the earth and carried it all the way to the Sky-God.

Nyame now called together all the elders of the skies, among them the Adonten, the Oyoko, the Kontire and Akwam chiefs, and informed them of the great exploits of Anansi, the spider:

'Many great warriors and chiefs have tried before,' the Sky-God told the congregation, 'but none has been able to pay the price I have asked of them. Kwaku Anansi has brought me Onini the python, the Mmoboro nest and the body of the mighty Osebo. The time has come to repay him as he deserves. He has won the right to tell my stories. From today, they will no longer be called stories of the Sky-God, but stories of Anansi, the spider.'

And so, with Nyame's blessing, Anansi became the treasurer of all the stories that have ever been told. And even now, whenever a man wishes to tell a story for the entertainment of his people, he must acknowledge first of all that the tale is a great gift, given to him by Anansi, the spider.

[1] The Ashanti refer to God as 'Nyame'. The Dagomba call him 'Wuni', while the Krachi refer to him as 'Wulbari'.

Anansi and the Corn Cob

(From the Krachi people, west Africa)

ANANSI WAS BY FAR THE CLEVEREST of Wulbari's heavenly creatures. He was also the most ambitious among them and was always on the look-out for an opportunity to impress the supreme god with his intelligence and cunning.

One day he appeared before Wulbari and asked if he might borrow from him a corn cob.

'Certainly,' said Wulbari, 'but what a strange thing to ask for! Why do you wish to borrow a corn cob?'

'I know it is an unusual request,' replied Anansi, 'but Master, if you will give me the corn cob I will bring you a hundred slaves in exchange for it.'

Wulbari laughed aloud at this response, but he handed Anansi the cob and declared that he looked forward to the day when the spider might deliver such a prize. Anansi meant every word he had spoken, however, and without further delay he set off on the road leading down from the sky to the earth.

It was nightfall by the time he completed his long journey and because he felt very weary, he went straightaway in search of a night's lodging. He soon happened upon the home of the village chief and having requested a bed, he was shown to a comfortable mattress in the corner of the room. But before he lay down to sleep he asked the chief where he might put the corn cob for safe-keeping:

'It is the corn of Wulbari,' Anansi explained. 'Our great Creator has instructed me to carry it to the people of Yendi, and I must not lose it along the way.'

The chief pointed to a hiding place in the roof and Anansi climbed up and placed the cob amongst the straw. Then he retired to his bed and pretended to be asleep. But as soon as the sound of the chief's snoring filled the room, Anansi arose again and removed the corn from its hiding place. He crept quickly out of doors and threw the corn to the fowls, making certain that the greedy birds helped themselves to every last kernel.

On the following morning, when Anansi asked for his corn, the chief climbed to the roof, but could not find any trace of it. Anansi stared at his host accusingly and began to create the most appalling scene, screaming and shouting and stamping his feet until, at last, each of the villagers was ordered to present him with a whole basket of corn each. This appeared to pacify Anansi only slightly, and very soon afterwards he took his leave of the chief declaring that he would never again visit such dishonest people.

He continued on his journey, carrying with him the great sack of corn he had collected. After a time he sat down by the roadside to rest and soon he spotted a man heading towards him carrying a chicken. Anansi greeted the man warmly and before long they had struck up a lively conversation.

'That's a nice, plump bird you have there,' Anansi said to the man. 'Nothing would please me more right now than to exchange my sack of corn for your fowl, for I am sick and weary of carrying my load from place to place.'

The man could scarcely believe his luck. There was enough corn in the bag to feed his entire family for several months and he very readily agreed to the exchange. The two shook hands and then went their separate ways, Anansi carrying the chicken under one arm, the man dragging the heavy sack behind him.

Later that day, Anansi arrived at the next village, and having asked the way to the chief's house, he knocked upon the door to beg a night's lodging. As before, the chief of the village welcomed him with open arms, and when Anansi showed him the fowl of Wulbari he had his people prepare a nice, quiet out-house where the bird could be placed out of harm's way overnight. But again, Anansi arose when he was certain everyone else had fallen asleep and killed the fowl, leaving the corpse in the bush and smearing some of the blood and feathers on the chief's own doorstep.

The next morning Anansi awoke and began shouting and thrashing about wildly.

'You have killed my precious fowl,' he shrieked as he pointed to the blood and the feathers. 'Wulbari will never forgive such a crime.'

The chief and all his people begged Anansi to forgive them and tried desperately to think of something that might appease him. At long last Anansi announced that perhaps there was something they could give him to take to the people of Yendi instead, and he pointed to a flock of sheep grazing in a nearby field.

'We will give you any number of these sheep if you will only pardon us,' said the chief.

So Anansi accepted the ten best sheep from the flock and went on his way once more.

It was not long before he reached the outskirts of Yendi, but before he entered the village he decided to allow his sheep to graze for a few minutes. And while he was seated on the grass watching them eat, he noticed a group of people approach, weeping and wailing as they returned home to their village bearing the body of a young man.

'Where are you taking the corpse?' Anansi asked them.

'We have a long way to go yet,' they told him, 'beyond those mountains to the west towards the dead boy's home.'

'But you look worn out,' said Anansi, 'I would be only too delighted to help you in any way. Here, take my sheep and lead them to your village and I will follow behind with the body on my shoulders.'

But Anansi allowed himself to fall further and further behind the men until finally they drifted out of sight. Then he retraced his steps and walked into the village of Yendi carrying with him the corpse. There he knocked on the door of the chief's house, explaining that he had with him the favourite son of Wulbari who was very weary from travelling and in desperate need of a bed for the night.

The chief and his people were delighted to have such an important guest among them and a comfortable hut was soon made ready for the favourite son of Wulbari. Anansi laid the body down inside the hut, covering it with a cloth before joining the chief for a splendid celebratory feast.

'I'm so sorry that our guest of honour is unable to join us,' said Anansi to the chief, 'but we have journeyed so far today, he has collapsed with exhaustion.'

The chief insisted that some of the best food be set aside for the son of Wulbari, and at the end of the evening he presented it to Anansi who promised to feed it to his companion as soon as he awoke. But Anansi finished the entire meal himself and sat cross-legged on the floor of the hut, chortling away to himself in the darkness.

At dawn, he called to the chief's own children to go in and wake the son of Wulbari.

'If he does not stir,' Anansi told them, 'you will have to flog him, for nothing else appears to wake him when he has slept so soundly.'

So the children did as they were instructed, but Wulbari's son did not wake.

'Beat him harder, beat him harder,' Anansi encouraged them, and the children did as he told them. But still Wulbari's son did not wake. So Anansi announced that he would go and wake the boy himself.

Soon there was a great wailing from inside the hut as Anansi cried out that the children of the chief had beaten to death the favourite son of Wulbari. The chief himself rushed forward and examined all the evidence. He was convinced that Anansi had spoken the truth and immediately offered to have his children sacrificed to the supreme god for what they had done to the unfortunate boy. But Anansi continued to wail aloud. Then the chief offered to kill himself, but still Anansi refused and said that nothing he could think of would ever undo such a great loss.

'Please just bury the body, I can't bear to look upon him any longer' he told the people. 'Perhaps when my mind is clearer I will think of some plan to appease Wulbari's anger.'

It was much later that same evening when Anansi reappeared, his eyes red and puffy from squeezing out the tears, his body stooped in mock-anguish.

'I have been thinking long and hard,' he said to the chief, 'and I have decided that I will take all the blame on myself for this dreadful deed, for I know you would never survive the wrath of Wulbari. I will say that his son's death was a terrible accident, but you must allow one hundred of your men to accompany me, for I will need them to support my testimony.'

The chief, who was more than pleased with this solution, immediately chose a hundred of the best young men and ordered them to prepare themselves for the long journey back to the kingdom of Wulbari. By midday they had departed the village and were well on the road leading upwards from the earth to the heavens.

Wulbari observed the crowd of youths approach and came out to greet them personally, anxious to discover their business, for he had forgotten all about Anansi and the bold promise he had made many weeks before.

'I told you it was possible, Master,' Anansi piped up from amongst the crowd. 'Do you not remember giving me that single corn cob? Now you have a hundred excellent slaves in exchange. They are yours to keep and I have kept my promise.'

Wulbari smiled broadly and was so pleased with Anansi he confirmed his appointment as Chief of his Host there and then, ordering him to change his name from Anyankon to Anansi, which is the name he has kept to the present day.

✳ ✳ ✳

Tortoise Fables

Tortoise and the Wisdom of the World

(From Nigeria, west Africa)

TORTOISE WAS VERY ANGRY when he awoke one day to discover that other people around him had started to behave just as wisely as himself. He was angry because he was an ambitious fellow and wanted to keep all the wisdom of the world for his own personal use. If he succeeded in his ambition, he felt he would be so wise that everyone, including the great chiefs and elders of the people, would have to seek his advice before making any decision, no matter how small. He intended to charge a great deal of money for the privilege, and was adamant that nothing would upset his great plan.

And so he set out to collect all the wisdom of the world before anyone else decided to help himself to it. He hollowed out an enormous gourd for the purpose and began crawling along on his stomach through the bush, collecting the wisdom piece by piece and dropping it carefully into the large vessel. After several hours, when he was happy he had gathered every last scrap, he plugged the gourd with a roll of leaves and made his way slowly homewards.

But now that he had all the wisdom of the world in his possession, he grew fearful that it might be stolen from him. So he decided straight away that it would be best to hide the gourd in a safe place at the centre of the forest. He soon found a very tall palm tree which seemed suitable enough and prepared himself to climb to the top. First of all he took a rope and made a loop around the neck of the gourd. When he had done this, he hung the vessel from his neck so that it rested on his stomach. Then he took a very deep breath and began to climb the tree.

But he found that after several minutes he had not made any progress, for the gourd was so large it kept getting in his way. He slung it to one side and tried again. Still he could not move forward even an inch. He slung the gourd impatiently to the other side, but the same thing happened. Finally, he tried to stretch past it, but all these efforts came to nothing and he beat the tree with his fists in exasperation.

Suddenly he heard someone sniggering behind him. He turned around and came face to face with a hunter who had been watching him with great amusement for some time.

Opposite: Tortoise decided it would be best to hide the gourd at the centre of the forest. He soon found a tall palm tree and prepared himself to climb to the top.

'Tortoise,' said the hunter eventually, 'why don't you hang the gourd over your back if you insist on climbing that tree?'

'What a good idea,' replied the tortoise, 'I'd never have thought of that on my own.'

But he had no sooner spoken these words when it dawned on him that the hunter must have helped himself to some of the precious wisdom.

Tortoise now grew even more angry and frustrated and began scuttling up the tree to get away from the thieving hunter. He moved so fast, however, that the rope holding the gourd slipped from around his neck causing the vessel to drop to the ground where it broke into hundreds of little pieces.

All the wisdom of the world was now scattered everywhere. And ever since that time nobody else has attempted to gather it all together in one place.

But whenever he feels the need, Tortoise makes a special journey to the palm tree at the centre of the forest, for he knows that the little pieces are still there on the ground, waiting to be discovered by anyone who cares to search hard enough.

The Tortoise and the Baboon

(From the Swahili speaking peoples, east Africa)

THE TORTOISE AND THE BABOON had been friends for a very long time and so it was only natural that they should invite each other to their wedding feasts when they both decided to get married.

The Baboon was the first to celebrate his wedding and he insisted that the feast be as elaborate as possible. The most delicious food was prepared by a team of twelve cooks, and the finest palm wine was provided for every guest.

Tortoise arrived punctually on the day and was most impressed by what he saw. He was extremely hungry after his very long journey, and more than anything he looked forward to tucking into the food in the company of the other guests.

At last the dinner gong was sounded and all the baboons began climbing the trees where they sat waiting to be served. Tortoise, of course, could not climb at all well and struggled very hard to make it even to the lowest branch. By the time he eventually reached the

Opposite: Tortoise was extremely hungry after his very long journey through the Great Falls, and more than anything he looked forward to tucking into the food.

party, the first half of the meal had been served and cleared and he found that he was ignored by the other guests who chatted loudly among themselves.

Finally, he thought it best to mention to his friend the slight problem he was having keeping his balance on the branch.

'But you must sit like the rest of us,' the Baboon told Tortoise, 'it is our custom. When my people eat, they always sit this way. It would be so rude to lie on the ground when everyone else is upright.'

And so Tortoise tried a little harder to make himself comfortable, but as soon as he reached forward to grab hold of some food, he fell flat on his belly. All the baboons roared with laughter at the sight of him and he hung his head in shame, feeling hungry and frustrated, knowing that he would never get to eat any of the delicious food.

When the day arrived for the Tortoise to marry, he had no wish to provide a lavish banquet for his guests, but prepared a small dinner-party for his closest friends. Before any of the guests were due to arrive, however, Tortoise went outdoors and lit a torch. Holding the flame to the earth, he began to burn the dry grass around his house and all the scrubland nearby.

Baboon and his new wife soon appeared in the distance and Tortoise slipped indoors again to resume the preparations. He embraced the couple warmly when they arrived and made sure that they were given one of the best seats at his table. The food was set down before them, and all were about to tuck in when Tortoise suddenly stood up and raised both arms in the air:

'Let's just make sure that we all have clean hands,' he said. 'Nothing upsets me more than people who eat their food with dirty hands.'

One by one his guests began to examine their hands, quite confident that they were clean. But when Baboon stared at his, he was shocked to see that they were a filthy black colour.

'But I scrubbed them before I left my house,' he protested.

'None the less,' replied Tortoise, 'they are very dirty indeed and it would be offensive to my people if you did not make an effort to clean them one more time. Go back to the river across the bush and try again. We promise to eat slowly so that you do not miss the meal.'

Baboon set off to do as his host suggested, walking on all fours through the charred grass and soot until he reached the river. Here he washed his hands thoroughly and returned by the same path to Tortoise's house.

Opposite:
'But you must sit like the rest of us,' the Baboon told Tortoise. 'It would be rude to lie on the ground when everyone else is upright.'

'But there is no improvement. You must go again,' said Tortoise, munching on a delicious yam. 'What a shame! We will have eaten everything if this keeps up.'

Again the Baboon returned and again the Tortoise sent him away, a third and a fourth and a fifth time, until all the splendid dishes had been gobbled up.

So in the end, Tortoise had his revenge, and for many years afterwards he took great delight in telling his friends the story of how he managed to outwit Baboon on his wedding day.

Tortoise and the Hot-water Test

(From the Yoruba people, west Africa)

EVERY YEAR AT HARVEST TIME, the chief called upon his people to help him gather in the crops. And every year, just as the work was about to commence, Tortoise disappeared to the country for a few weeks, for he was never very interested in lending a hand.

But there came a season when his own crops failed him and he began to worry about how he might survive the harsh winter ahead. Looking out through the window of his hut, he saw that the chief's fields were full of sweet yams and decided he would have to get his hands on enough of them to fill his empty storehouse.

Finally he came up with a plan. In the middle of the night, when nobody was looking, he took a large shovel and made his way to the chief's fields. He began to dig a very deep hole, broad at the base and narrow at the top. Then he scattered leaves and branches over the hole to hide it and crept back to his bed.

Early the next morning, Tortoise knocked upon the door of the chief's house.

'I have come to help you in the fields,' he told the chief, 'and I am prepared to stay as long as it takes, until every single yam has been harvested.'

Although very surprised, the chief was delighted with the extra pair of hands and sent Tortoise to join the others already hard at work filling their baskets. Opolo the frog had come to do his share, as had Ekun the leopard, Ekute the bush rat, Ewure the goat, and a great many more of the chief's people.

Tortoise watched for a few moments as each dug a yam, placed it in his basket and carried it to the chief's storehouse. He stooped and did the same for a while, making sure that his digging brought him closer and closer to the large hole he had made the night before. Then for every yam he placed in his basket, he began dropping one into the opening of the hole, slowly building a stockpile for himself and mopping his brow from time to time as if he were quite exhausted.

But some of the workers began to notice how little progress he was actually making and challenged Tortoise to increase his speed.

'Unlike the rest of you,' he answered them shortly, 'I have the greatest respect for the chief's yams and believe in handling them very gently so as not to bruise them.'

And so the work continued until at last all the yams were harvested and the people drifted home wearily to their supper.

That night, as soon as darkness fell, Tortoise led his wife and children to the spot where he had buried the yams. They tiptoed back and forth across the field many times, each carrying an armful of yams, until the hole was empty and the family storehouse was full. Tortoise was very pleased with himself. Everything had been taken care of, and he felt certain that he had more than enough food to last him through the winter months.

But when morning came, a group of the chief's servants, who had been touring the empty fields, stumbled upon the large hole Tortoise had dug. They also found footprints made by Tortoise and his family as they scurried to and fro during the night, and followed the footprints to Tortoise's storehouse. Carefully, they opened the door so as not to disturb the sleeping household, and there, piled high to the ceiling, they came face to face with an impressive mound of freshly harvested yams.

The servants immediately rushed back to the chief's house and reported to him their discovery. The chief was enraged to have been deceived in such a manner and ordered Tortoise to be brought before him at once.

'It has been reported to me that you have stolen yams from my field,' he challenged Tortoise, 'what have you got to say for yourself?'

'It really saddens me to think you have such a poor opinion of me,' replied Tortoise innocently, 'when I have gone out of my way to be of service to you. I went to your fields to work for you, I stooped and sweated and carried yams to your storehouse all day long. Now you reproach me and call me a thief.'

'Tortoise, your shrewd character is well known to me,' replied the chief, 'and you cannot argue your way out of this one as easily as you think. I have been told about the footprints leading from my fields to your storehouse.'

'Yes, I'm sure you have,' answered Tortoise confidently, 'but I could easily have made them when I returned home from my work. And besides, there were a lot of other people in the fields as well as myself.'

'There are no paths leading from my fields to their houses,' continued the chief, 'only to your house. But if you still insist you are innocent, I know of a way to prove it. Tomorrow you will take the hot-water test. Then we can put the matter to rest once and for all.'

The next day, the people gathered together in front of the chief's house where a large cauldron of water stood heating over a fire. As soon as the water had come to the boil, the chief appeared and began to address the crowd:

'You are assembled here to witness Tortoise take the hot-water test. He denies that he is guilty of theft. Therefore, he must drink a bowl of the boiling water. If he is innocent, he will feel nothing at all. But if he is guilty, the water will burn his throat and cause him great pain. Let us begin at once.'

But before the servants had ladled the water into the bowl, Tortoise spoke up:

'Sir, this test will only prove how faithful I have been to you and you will still be at a loss to know who has taken your yams. Don't you agree that it makes sense for everyone who worked alongside me in the fields to be tested as well?'

The chief considered this proposal a moment.

'Very well,' he said. 'Let everyone else who was in the fields come forward. I am sure they have nothing to hide and absolutely nothing to fear.'

And now Tortoise became very helpful, behaving as though he were the chief's special assistant. He ordered the pot to be removed from the fire and placed it in a spot where the chief would have a better view of the proceedings. Then he insisted, that because he was the youngest, he should respectfully serve the others before himself.

The chief agreed, and Tortoise took the bowl, filled it with boiling water and served it first of all to Opolo the frog. Opolo cried out in pain as the hot water burned his insides. Next came the bush rat and he too cried out in agony as the liquid scorched his throat.

Tortoise refilled the bowl and handed it to Ewure the goat. Tears came to his eyes also and he writhed on the ground as the pain consumed his entire body. Last of all, Ekun the leopard came forward and let out a piercing scream as he swallowed and suffered the same dreadful pain.

'You disappoint me, my friends,' said the chief, 'for I see that you all share a portion of the blame. But let us turn now to the Tortoise and see whether he is guilty or innocent.'

And so Tortoise stepped forward and filled his bowl to the brim. But before he held it to his lips he pushed it towards the chief:

'See how full it is, Sir,' he announced, 'I have taken more than anyone else.'

'I see it,' replied the chief, 'the amount is a good one.'

Tortoise carried the bowl towards the chief's wife.

'I see it also,' she cried, 'you have acted more than fairly, Tortoise.'

Tortoise walked slowly into the crowd and tilted the bowl so the men of the village could see it more clearly.

'We see it,' they said, 'the bowl is very full.'

He showed it to the women of the village.

'We see it,' they chanted, 'you are very brave indeed, Tortoise.'

He turned and called to all the children of the village.

'We see it,' they answered him, 'you do well, Tortoise.'

And as Tortoise presented the bowl for inspection to each group in turn, the water grew cooler and cooler until, at last, the chief called for him to get on with the drinking.

So Tortoise gulped down the water, but because it had grown so cool as he passed it around, it did not cause him any pain as it slid down his throat.

'You have seen it,' shouted Tortoise triumphantly, 'I did not cry out as the others did. How can I possibly be guilty?'

And as additional proof of his innocence, he poured the water over his entire body and rubbed it into his skin without showing any sign of discomfort.

'You can see it was not I who committed the crime,' he added. 'It must have been Opolo, Ekute, Ewure and Ekun. They should be taken away and punished severely.'

The chief nodded in agreement and sentenced the other animals to two years' hard labour on his farm for having stolen his yams.

But although Tortoise was victorious, there were some among the crowd who still held him in suspicion and ever since that day, whenever a person tries to point the finger at others for a crime he has committed himself, you will hear the people say:

'When Tortoise accuses the whole community,
He himself must have a great deal to hide.'

The Tortoise and the Elephant

(From the Akamba people, Kenya)

ONE DAY THE ELEPHANT WAS BOASTING as usual about his great size and strength.

'Have you ever come across a more impressive figure in the whole of the land?' he asked Tortoise, as he stared admiringly at his reflection in the lake. 'There is not one creature I know of that could outshine me. It wouldn't matter what sort of contest we were engaged in.'

'You can't be absolutely certain of that,' replied the Tortoise. 'Size isn't everything you know, and I'm sure there is someone out there who would put you in your place given half a chance.'

'I suppose you consider yourself worthy of that role,' mocked the Elephant. 'Come on then, prove to me that you are a greater athlete than myself.'

'That won't be so difficult,' answered the Tortoise defiantly. 'I bet I could jump as high as your trunk and land twenty feet beyond it without putting in too much effort.'

'Then meet me here later this afternoon,' the Elephant chuckled, 'and in the meantime go and work on your muscles! I can hardly wait to see you make a fool of yourself.'

So the Tortoise went home where he found his wife preparing their midday meal.

'The Elephant has challenged me to a trial of strength,' he told her, 'and I think it's time somebody taught him a lesson, but I will need your help.'

Leading his wife to the lakeside, Tortoise hid her among the bushes at exactly the spot where he judged he would land after making his miraculous leap. Soon afterwards, the Elephant arrived, still smirking to himself, and stood as he was instructed in the middle of a clear space where Tortoise could get a good run at him.

'Jump high now, Tortoise,' cried the Elephant sarcastically, 'give it your best shot.'

'I'm coming now, hold your trunk up high,' called the Tortoise, pretending he was almost ready for his high jump.

The Elephant lifted his head towards the sky, and as he did so, the tortoise slipped into the grass, shouting 'Hi-i!' as he went. 'Eh-e!' came the reply from his wife who suddenly appeared on the other side of the grass, exactly twenty feet from the Elephant.

The Elephant now glanced to his right and found the Tortoise on the far side of his trunk. He was utterly astonished to see him there and suspected nothing, believing that the leap had been so masterfully executed, his eyes had not been quick enough to take it in.

'You have beaten me, Tortoise,' he said, shaking his head in bewilderment, 'I still can't quite believe it, however. Do you think you could convince me one more time, for I feel certain that you would never be able to outrun me in a foot-race.'

'If you insist then,' answered the Tortoise quite casually, 'but not today. I need my rest after all that exertion. I will meet you tomorrow morning by the great tree in the forest, and to make things easier, I suggest we run a circular course through the woods, finishing up in the same place where we started from.'

'That sounds ideal,' replied the Elephant and he tramped his way homewards, confident that he would achieve his victory on the following day.

Before the sun had risen the next morning, Tortoise had gathered together his wife and children and spent several hours placing them along the course, instructing them what to do once the race had started. Shortly afterwards, he spotted the Elephant pushing his way through the thick undergrowth as he headed towards the appointed tree. Tortoise went forward to greet him and without further delay the two took up their starting positions, anxious to begin the race.

Smiling happily to himself, the Elephant trotted off at an easy pace and was soon well ahead of the Tortoise who began to puff and pant under the strain. The Elephant laughed loudly at the sight of him, well pleased with himself for having chosen such a punishing contest.

Opposite:
The Elephant boasted about his great size and strength. 'Have you ever seen a more impressive figure in the whole of the land?' he asked Tortoise.

When he had been running for quite some time he shouted back, 'Tortoise!', believing he had left his opponent far behind. But to his horror he heard a voice saying :

'Why are you looking behind you? I am here in front of you. Can't

you move any faster?'

Shocked by the sight of Tortoise, the Elephant broke into a gallop, putting as much energy into his stride as he could possibly manage. But he had only moved on a short distance when he spotted Tortoise up ahead of him once more. This happened again and again, all the way along the course, until the Elephant arrived back at the great tree where he found Tortoise calmly waiting for him, not a drop of sweat on his brow.

'Here I am, what kept you?' said the Tortoise.

'I didn't believe you could ever beat me,' replied the defeated Elephant, 'but it seems you are right about size.'

Tortoise turned away to hide his smile, but he never felt bad about cheating the Elephant, for he felt certain he had taught him an invaluable lesson.

Other Animal Stories

How the Leopard Got His Spots

(From Sierra Leone, west Africa)

LONG AGO, Leopard and Fire were the best of friends. Every morning, without fail, Leopard made a special effort to visit his friend even though the journey took him quite a distance from his own home. It had never before bothered him that Fire did not visit him in return, until the day his wife began to mock and tease him on the subject.

'He must be a very poor friend indeed,' she jeered, 'if he won't come and see you even once in your own house.'

Day and night, Leopard was forced to listen to his wife taunt him, until finally he began to believe that his house was somehow unworthy of his friend.

'I will prove my wife wrong,' he thought to himself, and set off before dawn on the following day to beg Fire to come and visit his home.

At first, Fire presented him with every possible excuse. He never liked to travel too far, he explained to Leopard. He always felt uncomfortable leaving his family behind. But Leopard pleaded and pleaded so that eventually Fire agreed to the visit on the condition that his friend construct a path of dry leaves leading from one house to the other.

Opposite: The bodies of Leopard and his wife were soon covered all over with black spots where the fingers of Fire, their reluctant house-guest, had touched them.

As he walked homewards, Leopard gathered as many leaves as he could find and laid them in a long line between the two houses just as Fire had instructed him. He brought his wife the good news and immediately she began to prepare the finest food to welcome their guest.

When the meal was ready and the house sparkled as if it were new, the couple sat down to await the arrival of their friend. They had been seated only a moment when suddenly they felt a strong gust of wind and heard a loud crackling noise outside their front door. Leopard jumped up in alarm and pulled open the door, anxious to discover who could be making such a dreadful commotion. He was astonished to see Fire standing before him, crackling and sparking in a haze of intense heat, his body a mass of flames that leapt menacingly in every direction.

Soon the entire house had caught fire and the smell of burning skin filled the air. Leopard grabbed hold of his squealing wife and sprang, panic-stricken, through the window, rolling in the grass to put out the flames on his back.

The two lay there exhausted, grateful to be alive. But ever since that day, their bodies were covered all over with black spots where the fingers of Fire, their reluctant house-guest, had touched them.

The Donkey Who Sinned

(From Ethiopia, north-east Africa)

ONE HOT AND SUNNY AFTERNOON, the Lion, the Leopard, the Hyena and the Donkey met together at the bottom of the field. At once, they began to discuss the drought visiting the country and the dreadful conditions that had become widespread throughout the region. No rain had fallen now for several months, the crops had shrivelled beyond recognition, and there was very little food or water to be had anywhere.

'How can this have happened to us?' they repeated over and over again, shaking their heads in disbelief. 'Someone among us must have sinned very badly, or God would not be punishing us in this way.'

'Perhaps we should confess our sins,' the Donkey suddenly suggested, 'maybe if we repent, we will be forgiven and the land will become fertile and bear healthy crops again.'

They all agreed that this was a very sensible idea, and so the Lion, the most powerful of the group, immediately stood up to make his confession:

'I once committed an unforgivable crime,' he told the gathering. 'One day I found a young calf roaming close to a village, and even though I knew it belonged to the people, I attacked it and ate every morsel.'

The other animals looked towards the Lion, whom they feared and admired for his daring and strength, and began to protest his innocence loudly:

'No, no,' they reassured him. 'That was no great sin! You shouldn't worry about that at all.'

Next the Leopard stood up to make a clean breast of things:

'I have committed a much more dreadful sin,' he announced. 'One morning as I prowled through the valley, I happened upon a goat who had strayed from the rest of the herd. As soon as his back was turned, I leaped on him and devoured him.'

The rest of the animals looked at the Leopard, whom they admired as a most ruthless hunter, and once again they dismissed this crime:

'No, no!' they insisted. 'That is no sin! God would never hold such a thing against you.'

The Hyena then spoke his piece:

'Oh, I have committed a most wicked deed,' he cried. 'I was so greedy one evening, I stole into the village, caught a chicken and

Opposite:
'I once committed an unforgivable crime,' said the Lion. 'One day I found a calf roaming close to the village. I attacked it and ate every morsel.'

⁂ 75 ⁂

swallowed it down in one gulp.'

But again the other animals protested, judging the Hyena to be the most cunning among their friends:

'No, no! Let your conscience be at rest,' they answered him. 'That is no sin!'

Last of all, the Donkey came forward and began to confess:

'One day when my master was leading me along the road, he met an old friend and started talking with him. While the two were deep in conversation, I crept silently to the edge of the road and began nibbling on a tuft of grass.'

The Lion, the Leopard and the Hyena stared at the Donkey, whom they neither feared, nor admired. A grave silence filled the air. Slowly they formed a circle around him, shaking their heads in absolute disgust:

'That is the worst sin we have ever heard,' they pronounced. 'There can be no doubt now that you are the source of all our trouble.'

And with that, the three of them jumped upon the donkey's back and began ripping him to pieces.

The Two Suns

(From Kenya, east Africa)

MANY HUNDREDS OF YEARS AGO, in the land now known as Kenya, the animals could speak just as well as human beings. At that time, the two species lived in harmony and agreed on most things. They even shared the same grievances, and were equally fond of complaining about the darkness, although they readily admitted that they were more than satisfied with the daylight.

'We cannot see at night,' complained the men. 'It is impossible to look after our cattle in the dark and we are often afraid of the great shadows that appear out of nowhere.'

The animals agreed with the men and soon they arranged a meeting to decide what to do. The great elders of the people were the first to speak and they outlined various plans to defeat the darkness, some suggesting that huge fires should be lit at night throughout the land, others insisting that every man should carry his own torch. At length, however, the man considered wisest among the elders stood up and addressed the crowd:

Opposite: The lion, the most powerful member of the group, was feared and admired by all the other animals.

'We must pray to God to give us two suns,' he announced. 'One that rises in the east and one that rises in the west. If he provides us with

these, we will never have to tolerate night again.'

The people immediately shouted their approval and all were in agreement with this plan, except for one small hare at the back of the crowd who ventured to challenge the speaker a little further:

'How will we get any shade?' he asked in a tiny voice.

But his question met with an impatient roar from the wisest elder who demanded to know the identity of the creature who had dared to oppose him.

'It was the Hare who spoke,' said one of the warriors in the crowd, noticing that the Hare was trying to hide himself away under the bushes. Soon he was hauled out to the middle of the gathering, visibly shaking under the gaze of the people.

'How dare you disagree with me,' said the elder. 'What do you know of such matters anyway?'

The Hare bowed his head silently and began to whimper.

'Speak up, great prophet,' said another of the elders. 'Let us hear your wise words of counsel.'

The people and the animals laughed loudly at the spectacle before them, all except for the warrior who had first spotted the Hare.

'Don't be afraid of them,' he said gently. 'Go on! Speak! Be proud of what you have to say.'

The Hare stared into the eyes of the tall warrior and his courage began to return. Then, clearing his throat and raising himself up on his hind legs, he spoke the following words:

'I only wanted to say that if we had two suns there would never be any shade again. All the waters of the rivers and lakes will dry up. We shall never be able to sleep and our cattle will die of heat and thirst. There will be fires and hunger in the land and we shall all eventually perish.'

The people listened and a great silence descended upon them as they considered the words of the little Hare.

At last, the wisest of the elders arose and patted the Hare warmly on the shoulder.

'Indeed you have shown greater wisdom than any of us,' he said. 'We are fortunate to have you among us.'

Everyone agreed, and to this day the people of Kenya say that the hare is the cleverest of all animals. And they still have day and night; they still have only one sun and nobody has ever complained about it since that day.

Gihilihili: The Snake-man

(From the Tutsi people, Rwanda)

THERE WAS ONCE A MIDDLE-AGED WOMAN living in a small village who for many years had tried to conceive a child. At last, when she had almost abandoned all hope, she discovered she was pregnant. The news filled her with great joy and she longed for the day when she could sit proudly amongst the other women holding her new-born infant in her arms.

But when nine months had passed and the time arrived for the woman to deliver her child, there was no sign of it emerging, and for several more years the infant remained within her womb, refusing to show itself. Eventually however, the woman began to suffer labour pains and was taken to her bed where she gave birth after a long and painful ordeal. She was surprised that her husband did not bring the infant to her and when she looked in his direction she saw that his eyes were filled with horror. Then she searched for the child, but no child lay on the bed. Instead she saw a long, thick-necked snake coiled up beside her, its body warm and glistening, its head lifted affectionately towards her.

Suddenly her husband grabbed hold of a shovel from a corner of the hut and began striking the snake furiously. But the woman cried out for him to stop at once:

'Do not harm the creature,' she pleaded, 'treat it with respect and gentleness. No matter what you may think of it, that snake is still the fruit of my womb.'

The man lowered his shovel and went outdoors. Soon he returned to the hut accompanied by a group of village elders. They gathered around the bed and began to examine the snake more closely. At length, the wisest among them spoke to the husband and wife:

'We have no reason to treat this creature unkindly,' he told them. 'Take it to the forest and build a house for it there. Let it be free to do as it pleases. Let it grow to maturity unharmed so that it may shed its skin in the normal way.'

The husband carried the snake to the heart of the forest and left it there as the elders had ordered him, making certain that it had a comfortable home to live in and a plentiful supply of food to survive on.

The years passed by quickly, and the snake grew to an impressive size, ready for the day when its old skin would be replaced by a new one. And as it wandered deeper into the forest the most wonderful transformation began to occur. The old skin started to shrink away to reveal a young man, tall, strong and handsome. The young man stood up and glanced around him. Then, lifting the

snakeskin from the ground, he took a deep breath and followed the path through the forest back towards his parents' home.

Both mother and father were overjoyed to discover that the snake-creature they had abandoned so many years before had changed into such a fine and handsome youth. All the other members of the family were invited to assemble at the hut to admire their beautiful son and a great feast was held to welcome him into the community.

After their son had been with them several weeks, the father sat down with him one evening to discuss who would make the best wife for him.

'I have already chosen the daughter of Bwenge to be my wife,' the young man told his father. 'Even while I crawled on my belly through the forests I knew I would one day marry her. Each time she came to gather wood, I sat and watched and my love went out to her. Each time she came to get water, my love went out to her. Each time she came to cut grass for the young cattle, my love went out to her.'

'You are not rich enough for such a match,' his father replied. 'We are poor people, and she is the daughter of a noble chief.'

But the son said nothing further on the subject and called for a great fire to be made. As soon as the flames had grown quite tall, he cast the snakeskin which once covered his body into the centre of the fire, calling for his father and mother to keep a careful watch on it. They looked on in amazement as the skin crackled noisily and transformed itself into an array of valuable objects. Cattle, sheep and fowls began to leap from the flames. Drums, calabashes and churns began to appear, together with all other kinds of wealthy possessions.

Next morning the father and his son went in search of the daughter of Bwenge and presented to the chief a selection of these goods. The chief was more than satisfied by all that he saw and arranged for his daughter to be married immediately. The young man led his new wife back to his village where he made a home for them both. They were very happy together and lived long and fruitful lives, enriched by the birth of many healthy children.

The Snake-man grew old among the people who came to regard him as a man of profound wisdom and courage. Whenever there was trouble they turned to him for advice, and even after he died, his words lived on in their memory and they often recounted the story of his birth, mindful of what he had told them.

'Never allow yourself to be destroyed by misfortune,' he had said.

'Never despair of yourself or of others. And above all, never condemn a person for his appearance.'

Opposite:
As the snake-creature wandered deeper into the forest, the most wonderful change occurred: the old skin started to shrink away to reveal a young man.

How the Dog Came to Live with Man

(From the Bushongo people, Congo)

THERE WAS A TIME, long ago, when the Dog and the Jackal lived together in the wilderness as brothers. Every day they hunted together and every evening they laid out on the grass whatever they had caught, making sure to divide the meal equally between them. But there were evenings when they both returned from a day's hunting empty-handed, and on these occasions they would curl up side-by-side under the stars dreaming of the bush calf or the plump zebra they had come so close to killing.

They had never before gone without food for longer than two days, but then, without warning, they suffered a long spell of bad luck and for over a week they could find nothing at all to eat. On the eighth day, although they had both searched everywhere, they returned to their shelter without meat, feeling exhausted and extremely hungry. To add to their misery, a bitterly cold wind blew across the bush, scooping up the leaves they had gathered for warmth, leaving them shivering without any hope of comfort throughout the long night ahead. Curled up together, they attempted to sleep, but the wind continued to howl and they tossed and turned despairingly.

'Jackal,' said the Dog after a while. 'Isn't it a terrible thing to go to bed hungry after all the effort we have put in today, and isn't it an even worse thing to be both hungry and cold at the same time?'

'Yes, it is brother,' replied the Jackal, 'but there's very little we can do about it at the moment. Let's just curl up here and try to sleep now. Tomorrow, as soon as the sun rises, we will go out hunting again and with any luck we will be able to find some food to satisfy us.'

But even though he snuggled up closer to the Jackal, the Dog could not sleep, for his teeth had begun to chatter and his stomach rumbled more loudly than ever. He lay on the cold earth, his eyes open wide, trying to recall what it was like to be warm and well-fed.

'Jackal,' he piped up again, 'man has a village quite close to this spot, doesn't he?'

Opposite: The Dog could not let go of the idea of approaching the village and began to imagine a delicious meal of the scraps and bones left lying around.

'Yes, that is true,' answered the Jackal wearily. 'But what difference can that make to us right now?'

'Well,' replied the Dog, 'most men know how to light a fire and fire would keep us warm if we crept near enough to one.'

'If you are suggesting that we take a closer look,' said the Jackal, 'you can forget about it. I'm not going anywhere near that village. Now go to sleep and leave me in peace.'

But the Dog could not let go of the idea and as he thought about it more and more he began to imagine the delicious meal he would make of the scraps and bones left lying around by the villagers.

'Please come with me,' he begged the Jackal, 'my fur is not as thick as yours and I am dying here from cold and hunger.'

'Go there yourself,' growled the Jackal, 'this was all your idea, I want nothing to do with it.'

At last, the Dog could stand it no longer. Forgetting his fear, he jumped up and announced boldly:

'Right, I'm off, nothing can be worse than this. I'm going to that village to sit by the fire and perhaps I'll even come across a tasty bone. If there's any food left over, I'll bring you some. But if I don't return, please come and look for me.'

So the Dog started off towards the village, slowing down when he had reached the outskirts and crawling on his belly so that nobody would notice him approach. He could see the red glow of a fire just up ahead and already he felt the warmth of its flames. Very cautiously he slid along the earth and had almost reached his goal when some fowls roosting in a tree

overhead began to cackle a loud warning to their master.

At once, a man came rushing out from a nearby hut and lifting his spear high in the air, brought it down within an inch of where the Dog lay.

'Please, please don't kill me,' whimpered the Dog. 'I haven't come here to steal your chickens or to harm you in any way. I am starving and almost frozen to death. I only wanted to lie down by the fire where I could warm myself for a short while.'

The man looked at the wretched, shivering creature and could not help feeling a bit sorry for him. It was such a cold night after all, and the Dog's request was not so unreasonable under the circumstances.

'Very well,' he said, withdrawing his spear. 'You can warm yourself here for a few minutes if you promise to go away again as soon as you feel better.'

The Dog crept forward and lay himself down by the fire, thanking the man over and over for his kindness. Soon he felt the blood begin to circulate in his limbs once more. Slowly uncurling himself, he stretched out before the flames and there, just in front of him, he noticed a fat and juicy bone, thrown there by the man at the end of his meal. He sidled up alongside it and began to devour it, feeling happier than he had done for a very long time.

He had just about finished eating when the man suddenly reappeared:

'Aren't you warm enough yet?' he asked, rather anxious to be rid of his visitor from the bush.

'No, not yet,' said the Dog, who had spotted another bone he wished to gnaw on.

'Just a few more minutes then,' said the man, as he disappeared inside his hut once more.

The Dog grabbed hold of the second bone and began crushing it in his strong jaws, feeling even more contented with himself. But soon the man came out of his hut and asked again:

'When are you going to get up and go? Surely you must be warm enough by now?'

But the Dog, feeling very reluctant to leave the comfort of his surroundings, pleaded with his host:

'Let me stay just a little while longer and I promise to leave you alone after that.'

This time the man disappeared and failed to return for several hours, for he had fallen asleep inside his hut, quite forgetting about his guest. But as soon as he awoke, he rushed out of doors to make certain that the Dog had left him as promised. Now he became angry to see the creature snoozing by the fire in exactly the same position as before. Prodding him with his spear, he called for the Dog to get up at once. The Dog rose slowly to his feet and summoning every ounce of his courage, he looked directly into the man's eyes and spoke the following words:

'I know that you want me to go away, but I wish you would let me stay here with you. I could teach you a great many things. I could pass on to you my knowledge of the wild, help you hunt the birds of the forests, keep watch over your house at night and frighten off any intruders. I would never harm your chickens or goats like my brother, the Jackal. I would look after your women and children while you were away. All I ask in return is that you provide me with a warm bed close to your fire and the scraps from your table to satisfy my hunger.'

The man now stared back into the Dog's eyes and saw that their expression was honest and trustworthy.

'I will agree to this,' he replied. 'You may have a home here among the villagers if you perform as you have promised.'

And from that day, the Dog has lived with man, guarding his property, protecting his livestock and helping him to hunt in the fields. At night when the Dog settles down to sleep, he hears a cry from the wilderness, 'Bo-ah, Bo-ah', and he knows that it is his brother, the Jackal, calling him back home. But he never answers the call, for the Dog is more than content in his new home, enjoying the comforts Jackal was once so happy to ignore.

The Truth about Cock's Comb

(From the Baganda people, central Africa)

THERE WAS A TIME, many years ago, when the wild cats of the forests were forced to live as servants of the fowls who frequently beat them and treated them with the utmost cruelty. The fowls, then the laziest of creatures, sat around preening their great feathers all day long, demanding that their servants supply them with food and anything else they might require. Whenever the cats caught flying ants, the fowls took four-fifths of them; whenever they had gathered millet seed, the fowls simply helped themselves to as much as they wanted. Of course, the cats did not like this arrangement, and often they considered rising up in rebellion. But one thing always held them back. They lived in fear of the scarlet combs the fowls wore on their heads, for they had been warned that if ever they came too close to them, they would be severely burnt and scarred for life.

One day, when it had turned bitterly cold, Mother Cat discovered that her fire had gone out, and knowing that her family would not survive very long without heat, she made a brave decision to send her youngest son to the fowls to beg for fire. When the young cat arrived at the home of the Head Cock he found him stretched out on the floor of his hut, quite alone, and apparently very drunk. The young cat approached the Head Cock cautiously and announced the purpose of his visit in a tiny, terrified voice. But he received no response whatsoever as the cock continued to snore very loudly. Once more he tried, raising his voice ever so slightly, but still there was no answer.

So the young cat went back home and told his mother that he had tried to wake the cock without any success.

'You must go back there again,' his mother told him. 'And this time, take some dry grass with you. If you find that the cock is still asleep, stick a blade of grass into his comb and bring me back the fire.'

The young cat set off once more to do as his mother had bid him. When he arrived at the Head Cock's hut, he found he had not moved an inch. Slowly he crept towards the sleeping figure and, ever so carefully, touched the comb with the grass. But surprisingly, there was no sign of any fire, not even a spark, and the blade of grass remained quite as cold as it had ever been.

Again, the young cat returned home and told his mother what had happened.

'You can't have tried hard enough,' she scolded. 'I suppose I will have to abandon the rest of the children and come along with you this time.'

And so for the third time, the young cat set off towards the Head Cock's hut, accompanied by his mother who was determined to have her fire at any price. Luckily, the cock continued to snore as before and it was not difficult for Mother Cat to approach him and touch his comb with the grass. Gently she blew on the stalk, expecting it to burst into flame. But the result was exactly as her son had described it – there was no fire, no spark, not even the slightest glimmer of heat.

Mother Cat was now rather perplexed, and even though she was afraid of being burnt, she decided to risk placing her hands on the cock's comb to see if it was hot. Slowly and carefully she stretched out her fingers, but as soon as they rested on the scarlet comb, she found that it was stone cold.

At first astonished by the discovery, Mother Cat became very angry as she contemplated the long years of suffering her family had endured under Head Cock and the rest of the fowls. She began shaking the drunken creature violently and as soon as he had awoken she dragged him to his feet.

'We don't fear you anymore,' she screamed at him. 'We tested your comb while you were asleep and we know that you have deceived us all. There is no fire in it and there never has been. Now, if you value your life, you had better leave this place as quickly as you can.'

The Head Cock saw that his empty boasting had been discovered and fled from his village as fast as his legs could carry him. And ever since that time, fowls have been forced to take refuge with man, squawking in fear whenever they think a cat is coming too close to them.

Chameleon Wins a Wife

(From the Kikuyu people, Kenya)

ONE DAY FROG SWAM to the surface of a little pond and glanced around him for a place to rest:

'The water is cold today,' he complained, 'it would do me good to bask in the sun for a little while.'

And so he left the water and crouched on a warm, flat stone at the edge of the pond.

After some time a beautiful young girl from the local village named Ngema came to the pond to fetch some water. The Frog remained seated on the stone without moving a muscle so that the young woman eventually began to stare at him, asking herself aloud whether or not he might be ill.

'No, I am not ill,' Frog called to her irritably, 'why do you imagine such a thing? Can't you see how strong I am?'

'Other frogs usually leap back into the water as soon as they see the villagers approach,' replied the girl, 'but you don't seem at all frightened and that is why I thought perhaps you must be sick.'

The Frog turned his two big eyes towards Ngema, rose up on his hind legs and stretched himself impressively towards the sky.

'Underneath this body, I am really a fine young man,' he boasted.

'I have enough cattle and goats to buy any number of beautiful girls like yourself, but a curse rests on me and I must remain here until it is lifted.

'When my father lay on his death bed, he said to me: "My son, you will spend most of your time by the water until the day comes when you meet a girl there and ask her to marry you. If she accepts, it will mean happiness for you both, but if she refuses, she will die." So I ask you to marry me here and now, and it is entirely up to you whether you live or die.'

The girl sat down on the grass and began thinking hard. After a while she stood up again and answered the Frog worriedly:

'If that curse rests on you, then it rests on me as well. I have seen you and you have asked me to be your wife. I will not refuse you now, for I have no wish to die just yet.'

So Ngema reluctantly agreed to marry the Frog and led him home to her parents' hut on the outskirts of the village.

In the courtyard at the front of her parents' house there stood a very beautiful palm tree. Among its broad, leafy branches sat a Chameleon watching the approach of the young girl and the Frog. Ngema escorted her companion indoors and left him there to discuss the wedding arrangements with her father while she sat down at the base of the tree to grind some corn for the midday meal. The Chameleon now moved cautiously towards her, descending from branch to branch slowly and carefully, his eyes darting suspiciously from side to side, until at last he stood within a few feet of her. But before he had the opportunity to address the girl, she suddenly turned towards him:

'I have been watching you all this time,' she said, 'and I can scarcely believe how long it took you to move such a short distance. Do you know that it has taken you over an hour to reach this spot?'

'I won't apologise for that,' answered the Chameleon. 'I am a stranger to you, and had I rushed upon you, you would have been frightened and called out to your people. But in this way I haven't alarmed you and now we will be able to talk quietly without anyone disturbing us.'

'I have been so anxious to meet you, but wanted to choose my moment carefully. I came here early this morning to tell you I love you and my greatest wish is for you to become my wife.'

The young girl set aside her bowl of corn and fell silent for several moments. At length, she raised her head and answered the Chameleon rather indifferently:

'You are too late with your request, and besides, I could never marry anyone who moves as slowly as you do. People would laugh to see us together.'

'Our elders say that empty gourds make a great noise, but it amounts to very little in the end,' replied the Chameleon. 'Think again before you reject me.'

Ngema sighed deeply as she pondered these words.

'Well,' she said finally, 'Frog is inside the house asking my father's permission to marry me. Whichever of you can satisfy him will earn the right to become my husband.'

So Chameleon waited for Frog to emerge and then entered the house to see if he could reason with the young girl's father. Their conversation was not half so difficult as Chameleon had expected and before long he reappeared smiling to himself, having agreed with the old man that he would return to claim his bride within a few days.

As soon as he had put all his affairs in order, Chameleon returned as promised to the girl's home, anxious to get on with the wedding ceremony. But to his disgust, he found Frog still pleading for Ngema's hand, insisting that he was by far the richer of the two, and that he would make a much more suitable husband.

Chameleon stormed into the room and interrupted Frog in mid-stream:

'You call me a slow and worthless creature,' he yelled furiously, 'but I call you a slippery, boneless, hideous carbuncle.'

And the two continued to hurl abuse at each other for some time, each of them determined to prove their worth before the young girl's family.

At last, the old man called for them both to stop and when they were ready to listen he offered them the following solution:

'I will fix a bride-price,' he told the pair, 'which must be delivered before the end of six days. The first of you to arrive here with everything I demand will win my daughter's hand in marriage.'

Then the old man listed out the various goods he desired from each of them and without further discussion Frog and Chameleon went their separate ways, eager to assemble their respective cargoes as hastily as possible.

The Frog enlisted a great number of his friends to help him and overnight he had prepared a vast quantity of beer and food of every kind, including sweet potatoes, corn, dove-peas, shea-nuts and bananas, which he piled on to an enormous caravan ready to take to the girl's house.

Early the next morning, a long line of frogs began hopping down the road, travelling at great speed in order to ensure that they would reach their destination before the Chameleon. But as they moved along, they began to attract the sniggers of the roadside workers, for they failed to notice that at every hop, the beer spilt from the gourds, the bananas dropped from the baskets, and the food crumbled to pieces in the open bags and fell to the ground.

When the company approached Ngema's house, they received a very warm welcome from the large crowd who set off to meet them. Songs of praise were sung by the women of the village and a loud chorus of cheering could be heard for miles around. But when, later that same evening, the villagers eventually came to unfasten the loads, they were horrified to see that all the sacks were completely empty and not a drop of beer remained in the gourds. The villagers called the father of the girl and reported to him their discovery:

'Come and examine the gifts Frog has brought you,' they told him, 'he has arrived here with empty sacks and dry bowls.'

The old man looked at the Frog sternly and raised his voice in anger:

'Why have you come here to mock us? Do you think I would exchange my precious child for such a worthless cargo? Go and seek a wife elsewhere, for I have no time for a son-in-law who would attempt to trick me like this.'

The Frog did not pause to argue his case, for he knew that his impatience and arrogance had cost him his bride and that now the curse would never be reversed. He hung his head in shame and silently slunk away, hopping despondently down the road with the rest of his companions.

Three more days passed by and most of the villagers had abandoned all hope that Chameleon would ever show his face among them. But then, from the opposite direction on the fifth morning, the people spotted a caravan of carriers making very slow progress towards the village. It was mid-afternoon by the time it reached the outskirts, and as before, the villagers went forward to welcome their guests.

But this time, the women of the village were very anxious to inspect the loads before disturbing the father of the bride. They approached the caravan warily, but their fears were quickly laid to rest, for as soon as they began to unwrap the cargo, they found the sacks overflowing with food and the gourds full to the brim with beer.

Ngema smiled as she moved forward to greet the Chameleon, remembering how he had once described to her the hollow sound of an empty gourd. The celebrations now began in earnest and the satisfied father gave his daughter to the victorious Chameleon who took her for his wife the very next day.

Opposite:
Three more days passed by and most of the villagers had abandoned all hope that Chameleon would ever show his face among them.

* * *

STORIES OF WIT AND WISDOM

tories which explore human experience – man's strengths and weaknesses, his relationship with his fellow beings and his correct place within society, form an intrinsic part of the African mythological tradition.

Many of the stories included in this chapter may be described as 'proverbial'. They offer instruction, often culminating in some form of moral punch line, which demonstrates well the African storyteller's use of tales as a vehicle to teach man correct social values, responsibility, humility, and a sense of justice.

The tales are chosen from different regions of Africa and are widely known. 'The Young Man and the Skull', for example, a story which recurs in several different versions all over the African continent, is characteristic of the group. It embodies a simple proverb, linked to the protagonist's unhappy fate, warning us that boastfulness is a sign of moral decadence which cannot go unpunished. Similarly, 'The Rich Man and the Poor Man' demonstrates the fact that greed will never be rewarded.

Other stories, among them 'How Walakuga Answered the King' and 'The Two Rogues', have a less serious intention and focus rather more light-heartedly on man's cunning, commending it as an essential tool for his survival.

The Rich Man and the Poor Man

(From the Akamba people, Kenya)

IN A CERTAIN VILLAGE OF THE AKAMBA there lived two men, one rich and one poor. Yet in spite of their different circumstances, they lived together as neighbours. The rich man always supported his poor friend in times of trouble and in return, the poor man worked hard on the rich man's farm, ploughing the fields and carrying out as many odd jobs as he could manage.

But there came a time when a severe famine spread throughout the land, causing widespread hardship and misery. Even the rich man could not escape the suffering, and as he watched his wealth decline, he grew hard-hearted towards his fellow men. Soon he had forgotten all about the poor man and when, one day, his old friend arrived on his doorstep to beg the scraps from his table, the rich man dismissed him as a common beggar and warned him never to trespass on his land again.

The poor man watched his children die of starvation one by one until only himself and his wife remained. But even though his spirit was almost broken, he was determined to keep his wife alive, and so he swallowed his pride and set off one evening towards the village where he began searching through other people's waste for even an old bone to chew on. Before long, he was approached by a well-dressed woman who took pity on him and presented him with a handful of maize. The poor man carried the maize home to his wife and she set a great pot of water over the fire to boil. She had intended to make a hot, nourishing soup for them both, but this proved an impossible task, since they had no meat to add to the broth and no salt with which to season it.

The poor man sat at his table trying to figure out how he might improve the flavour of his meal when suddenly an idea came to him he thought might be worth trying.

'I wonder if my rich friend is having a nice dinner tonight,' he said to himself, and he promptly arose from the table and set off in the direction of the rich man's farmhouse. He crept close enough to take a good look through the kitchen window and there, right in front of him, he saw a steaming-hot chicken lying on a plate of thick gravy. The delicious smell of the cooked meat wafted on the breeze towards him, causing the poor man's stomach to grumble loudly. Without wasting another second, he rushed back to his hut, grabbed his bowl of watery soup, and sat down against the outside wall of the rich man's house. Then, as he spooned the thin liquid down his throat, he breathed in the aroma of the meat and began to imagine that he was chewing on the most tender pieces of chicken flesh. When he had finished his meal, he felt very satisfied and hurried off home to tell his wife how clever he had been.

A few days later, the poor man saw the rich man and could not prevent himself boasting of his cleverness once again.

'I came to your house a few days ago,' he told the rich man, 'and while I drank my watery soup I breathed in the delicious smell rising up from your table. I might as well have sat alongside you sharing the same chicken. My own meal tasted equally good.'

'So that is why my food tasted so dull,' roared the rich man, 'you stole all its flavour from me. Well, you must pay for what you have taken. I order you to come with me to the judge. We will let him decide your punishment.'

The poor man was hauled that same day before the judge who ordered him to pay one goat to the rich man for having stolen the aroma from his food. But the poor man could not even afford to pay the rich man a single grain of wheat, let alone a goat, and he drifted slowly homewards, his head bowed in despair, wondering how he could possibly break the distressing news to his wife.

While he walked towards his hut, he met a wise old man hobbling along the road. And as the two were headed in the same direction, they soon struck up a conversation. The poor man revealed to his companion the whole sad story of what had happened and the wise man agreed with him that he had been most unfairly treated.

'I have a goat I will give you,' said the old man, 'I will go and fetch it for you. Take it home and look after it until the day you are called upon to make your payment. When that day arrives, I promise I will reappear to help you.'

And saying this, the wise man went off to fetch the goat, leaving the poor man a little bewildered, yet relieved to know that all was not entirely lost.

Less than a week later, the judge sent a message to the poor man telling him that he should appear before him to deliver the promised payment. By midday a large group of people had gathered in front of the judge's house to witness the proceedings. At the centre of the crowd stood the wise man, listening intently to all that was said. He behaved as if he knew nothing of the whole affair and began asking the people to explain to him what was happening.

'The poor man is supposed to pay the rich man a goat for having stolen the smell from his food,' they told him.

'But why make so much fuss over such a trivial incident?' the wise man asked.

'The poor man must pay the rich man his goat,' the people repeated, 'that is the judge's decision and we must stand by it.'

'And would you accept another judgement on this case?' the old man enquired politely.

'We would,' replied the people, 'if you can prove yourself a good enough judge.'

So the old man moved forward to the front of the crowd and addressed the people with the following words:

'A man who steals should be forced to repay only as much as he has taken. If the poor man had eaten the food, he should be made to pay back that food. But if he has only breathed the smell, he should only pay back the smell, nothing more, nothing less.'

'Yes, that is very true,' answered the people, 'but how can a man give back just the smell of the food?'

'I will show you a way,' answered the wise man. Then he turned to the rich man and said to him:

'The goat you have asked for has been brought to you. But you may not have it unless the poor man has taken your food. Beat this goat with your staff instead and when the animal bleats, take the sound of its bleating as payment for the smell of your food. Surely you will agree with me that this is a fair exchange!'

The rich man could not argue against this judgement and all around him the people began to clap their hands, delighted to have experienced such wisdom at first hand.

And so the poor man was saved from an unfair sentence and was allowed to go home. But the rich man was made to appear a selfish and greedy individual before the entire village. He slunk away silently and hoped that the whole affair would blow over, but whenever he appeared again in public, the people pointed at him and whispered among themselves:

'He who rides the horse of greed at a gallop will be forced to dismount at the door of shame.'

How Walukaga Answered the King

(From the Baganda people, central Africa)

WALUKAGA, THE BLACKSMITH, was by far the most gifted craftsman in the village, capable of turning his hand to all kinds of metalwork. Every morning a crowd usually gathered at his home, gasping in amazement at the speed with which he produced spears and axes, shovels and hoes, armlets and collars, and a whole variety of objects for the benefit of the villagers. The blacksmith's fame had spread far and wide so that even the king took a particular interest in his work and lined his courtyards with wonderful iron figures Walukaga had created specially for him.

One day a messenger from the palace arrived at the blacksmith's home to announce that the king wished him to perform a very special task. Walukaga was delighted by the news, for nothing pleased him more than to serve the king with his craft. He hurried off into a back room where he put on his finest crimson robe and a beautifully decorated head-dress. Then he followed the messenger to the palace, trying to imagine as he went along what kind of exciting work lay in store for him.

He was immediately shown to the king's private chamber and as soon as the king clapped his hands a group of servants appeared carrying several trays of iron pieces in various shapes.

'I have a very special job for you, Walukaga,' the king announced enthusiastically. 'I was staring at those fine figures you made for me just the other day when it occurred to me how nice it would be to have a life-size metal man for a companion. But I don't just mean a statue. What I want is an iron man who can walk and talk, who has blood in his veins, wisdom in his head and feelings in his heart.'

Walukaga almost collapsed with the shock. He stared long and hard into the king's eyes looking for a sign that the whole thing was some kind of joke, but the king's stern expression filled him with despair. From that moment onwards, the blacksmith had no peace of mind, for he well knew that failure to obey his sovereign's wishes would certainly mean death for himself and his family.

'I will do my very best to please you,' he answered mournfully and arranged for the iron to be delivered to his forge later that same day.

Next morning, Walukaga arose earlier than usual and made a tour of the neighbouring houses hoping that someone among his friends would be able to help him out of the terrible situation he now found himself in.

But every last person he turned to for advice could only offer the most impractical suggestions. One friend recommended that he build a metal shell and put a real man inside it, refusing to believe that the king would ever notice the difference. Another suggested that he flee the country and remain in hiding until the whole affair had been forgotten, entirely overlooking the fact that Walukaga had a wife and children to think of. A third even advised him to persuade the palace cook to poison the king's food. Walukaga listened to each neighbour in turn and fell into a deep depression. He returned home in the afternoon and shut himself away in his room, knowing that his days were numbered and trying desperately hard to come to terms with that fact.

A few days later, as Walukaga walked through the bush deep in thought, he managed to stray from his usual path and found himself wandering through a deserted stretch in search of a familiar landmark. Suddenly he thought he heard voices up ahead and moving closer to investigate, discovered a filthy-looking man sitting cross-legged on the ground chatting away to himself. The blacksmith recognized the man as someone once well-known in the village who had suffered so much misfortune as a youth he had gone completely mad and taken refuge in the wilderness.

Although frightened at first, Walukaga soon realized that the madman was in fact perfectly harmless and decided to accept the cup of water offered him as a sign of friendship. Soon the pair began chatting, and as the conversation turned to more important things, the blacksmith felt he would have nothing to lose if he unburdened himself and told the madman all about the king's impossible command. His companion sat and listened quietly to the very end without interruption and when Walukaga, only half-seriously, asked him whether he had any advice to spare, he was surprised to see the madman's eyes narrow almost to a squint and his face take on a grave and purposeful expression.

'I will tell you precisely what you should do,' the madman spoke clearly and decidedly. 'I want you to go to the king and tell him if he really wants you to make this remarkable iron man, you must have only the very finest materials. Say to him that you will need a very special charcoal and a plentiful supply of water from a most unusual source. Let him send word to the people of the village that they must shave their heads and burn their hair until they have produced a thousand loads of charcoal, and let him order them to weep into their water-

Opposite: From the moment he had heard the king's request, Walukaga had no peace of mind, for he knew that failure would almost certainly mean death.

bowls until they have given him a hundred pots of tears.'

The blacksmith pondered this advice and rapidly concluded it was by far the best he had received to date. But when he turned to thank the madman, he saw that he had begun rocking back and forth, laughing hysterically and shaking his head uncontrollably. Walukaga felt he had no more time to lose, and in spite of the late hour, he hurried off towards the palace, anxious to say his piece before his courage failed him.

Bowing low before the king, he timidly listed off all the things he would need to complete the work requested of him. But the king listened patiently and agreed to everything demanded, promising that the materials would be collected as smoothly and swiftly as possible.

So the very next day, messengers were sent out to every part of the kingdom ordering the people to shave their heads and weep into their bowls. Nobody dared disobey the king's command and even the women and children came forward without complaint. The people did their very best to comply with the king's wishes, but after seven days, when all of them had shaved their heads and wept until their eyes were red and raw, there was still not enough charcoal to make up even a single load, or enough tears to fill half a water-pot.

The elders of the kingdom had little choice but to appear before their leader and confess to him their lack of success. But as they stood before the king, quaking at the thought of the punishment he would deal them, they were relieved to discover that his response was more than reasonable. The king accepted that the people's efforts had been sincere and he sighed deeply and sent for the blacksmith to appear before him.

'Walukaga,' he said, 'you may stop your work on the iron man I asked you to build me. You have requested something impossible and my people cannot deliver the materials you need. Go home now and continue on with the work you are best at.'

Walukaga approached the king and smiled a little nervously.

'I hope you will not be angry with me, Your Majesty,' he said, 'but because you asked the impossible of me, I knew I had to do the same in return. I could never have made you a living man of iron, no more than your people could have delivered the charcoal and the water I demanded.'

But the king was not in the least bit angry, for he was delighted to have such a clever and honest man among his subjects.

The Young Man and the Skull

(From the Mbundu people, south-west Africa)

ONE DAY A YOUNG HUNTER had journeyed far into the bush in search of antelope when he accidentally stumbled upon a skull lying in the earth. Drawing nearer, he stooped to the ground to examine the object and began muttering to himself:

'How did you manage to get here my friend? What can have brought you to this unhappy end?'

To the young man's absolute astonishment, the skull opened its jaws and began speaking:

'Talking brought me here, my friend. Talking brought me to this place.'

The hunter raced back towards his village to tell the people all about his discovery.

'Friends,' he cried excitedly, 'I have just come across a human skull in the bush and it has spoken to me. It must be a wonderful sign.'

'Nonsense,' they replied, 'how can you possibly hold a conversation with the head of a dead man?'

'But it really did speak to me,' the young man insisted, 'you only refuse to believe me because you are jealous.'

But still the people continued to jeer him.

'Why not go and tell the chief all about your discovery,' one mocked, 'I'm sure he'll be overjoyed by the news!'

'I will do precisely that,' retorted the young man angrily, and off he marched towards the chief's house to tell him all about the skull.

But the chief, who had been taking his afternoon nap, was extremely unhappy that he had been disturbed.

'Why have you come here with your tall stories?' he shouted. 'You had better be telling the truth or I will see to it that your own head comes off. Now, take me to this wretched place and let me hear the skull's message for myself.'

A small crowd set off from the village, arriving shortly afterwards at the place where the young man had made his discovery. And sure enough, they soon spotted the skull sitting in the earth.

'It looks perfectly ordinary,' complained the people after a time, 'when are we going to hear it speak?'

The young man crouched to the ground and repeated the words he

had first spoken to the skull. But no answer came and the skull's jaws remained firmly shut. Again, the hunter spoke to it, raising his voice more loudly, but only silence followed.

Now the crowd began to grow restless and when a third and fourth attempt produced exactly the same result, they leapt on the young man and chopped off his head as the chief had ordered.

The head fell to the ground and rolled alongside the skull. For a long time afterwards all remained quiet as the villagers disappeared over the hill bearing the body homewards for burial. Then the skull opened its jaws and spoke up:

'How did you manage to get here my friend? What can have brought you to this unhappy end?'

'Talking brought me here,' replied the head. 'Talking brought me to this place.'

The Story of the Glutton

(From the Bantu speaking peoples, east Africa)

SEBGUGUGU WAS A POOR MAN who lived with his wife and children in one of the shabbiest huts in the village. He had very few possessions worth speaking of and certainly nothing of any great value to his name, apart from a white cow and calf he had inherited from his bride many years before on their wedding day.

One morning, as Sebgugugu sat outside his hut lazing in the warm sunshine, he observed a brightly coloured bird hopping towards him. The bird drew closer and, perching itself on the gate-post, began to chirp a little song. Sebgugugu listened attentively, and after a time he became convinced that the bird was speaking to him through the melody.

'Kill the White One,' he heard it say. 'Kill the white one and you will get a hundred in return.'

Sebgugugu stood up excitedly and called to his wife across the fields to come and hear the strange song. Obediently, she stopped her work and hurried back towards the hut. But after she had listened to the bird singing for a few minutes she turned and said to her husband:

'I cannot hear anything unusual. It is only a sweet little song. Perhaps you have had too much hot sun for one day.'

'That bird is definitely speaking to us,' her husband argued,

Opposite:
'You have left us little choice but to abandon our home and roam the countryside in search of food for ourselves and the children.'

'and I'm certain he is trying to deliver a message from the great Imana[1]. He is telling us that we will get a hundred fat cows if only we kill the white one we own.'

'Surely you would never consider doing such a thing!' his wife cried out in alarm. 'We depend on that cow for milk to feed our children and if anything happens to it they will die of starvation.'

But Sebgugugu chose to ignore these words and marched off, axe in hand, towards the field to kill the white cow.

That evening, the family feasted on freshly roasted beef and for several weeks afterwards they had enough food to keep them satisfied. Soon, however, the meat began to run out and their stomachs felt very empty. There was still no sign of the hundred cows intended to replace the one they had slaughtered, but Sebgugugu would not accept any of the blame for this and carried on as before, basking lazily in the sun while his wife struggled to feed their children and keep the household together.

A few weeks later, the strange bird made a second visit to Sebgugugu's hut and this time he heard it advise him to kill the calf of the white cow. Though his wife pleaded with him, Sebgugugu went ahead as before and slaughtered the young animal, cutting up the carcass for food. But there was far less meat on this occasion, and it lasted only a few days. The children, thirsty without milk, and hungrier than ever, began to grow pale and thin. And when he saw that the hundred cows had still failed to appear, Sebgugugu became slightly fearful for the first time.

'The children are starving,' he said to his wife anxiously, 'there is nothing else here for them to eat.'

'Didn't I warn you this would happen when you slaughtered the first of our precious cattle,' his wife replied angrily. 'You have left us with little choice now but to abandon our home and roam the countryside in search of food.'

Next morning, the family gathered together what few belongings remained in their hut and started off in search of food. By midday, they had travelled a long distance and sat down by the roadside to recover their strength. Weary and footsore, Sebgugugu buried his head in his hands, ready to give up the fight:

'What can I do to save my children?' he cried out despondently. 'I have been a very foolish creature.'

But the Great Creator, Imana, who had been watching over the family from above, now appeared before the sobbing man and spoke to him encouragingly:

'What is your trouble, Sebgugugu?' he enquired. 'You should know by now that you have only to ask and I will do my best to help you.'

Sebgugugu raised his eyes and confessed to the High God every detail of his selfish behaviour.

'I can see that you are sorry,' Imana responded, 'and I will give you the chance to prove to me that you are a man of worth. Walk towards that cattle-kraal beyond the hill and there you will find an old crow guarding the herd. Say to him that I have given you permission to drink the milk. Do not forget to thank him for his hospitality and remember to treat him always with the utmost respect.'

Sebgugugu promised to do all this and headed off towards the kraal. He could not find any trace of the old crow when he arrived, but his eyes soon lit up at the sight of four large churns standing nearby, full to the brim with creamy, white milk. Sebgugugu bent over the milk and helped himself to as much as he wanted, leaving just about enough for his wife and children.

Suddenly, in the distance, he caught sight of the old crow driving the cattle homewards, flying back and forth and squawking over their heads to keep them together. Remembering what Imana had said, Sebgugugu ran forward to greet the herdsman, apologizing for the fact that his wife had drunk so much of the milk.

'But I will see to it that she repays you in some way,' he reassured the crow. And as the two of them sat down to chat for the evening, he ordered his wife to fetch a pail and begin milking the cows. When she had done this, he ordered her to build a fire to drive the mosquitoes away. Then, he instructed her to bring the crow a bowl full of milk for his supper. Although exhausted, his wife performed all of these tasks without complaint, grateful for the fact that her children had found a place of refuge where they could be restored to health under the crow's protection.

For a long time, things went on well in this way, but then, without warning, Sebgugugu began to grow restless and discontented.

'That old crow is beginning to annoy me,' he said to his wife one day. 'There really couldn't be a better time to do away with him, you know. Our own children are now old enough to herd the cattle for me, so we really have no use for him anymore.'

His wife was appalled to hear him say such a thing, but although she protested loudly, Sebgugugu took his bow and arrows and went outdoors to lie in wait for the crow as he returned home with the cattle that evening. When the crow came near enough, he took aim and shot an arrow in his direction. But the arrow missed its target and the startled crow took to the skies. As he did so, the cattle began to disappear into thin air one by one until there was not so much as a stray calf remaining to satisfy the needs of the family. Sebgugugu looked to his wife for comfort, but she could not give him any. Reduced to destitution once more, she led her children by the hand along the road away from the kraal, her head bowed in disappointment and misery.

They had not gone very far, however, before the benevolent Imana appeared before them once more.

'You have behaved very badly,' he chastised Sebgugugu, 'but I am prepared to give you another chance. If you walk a little deeper into the bush you will come across a long, twisted vine lying in the earth. Sprinkle a little water on the vine, and soon you will be able to gather from it not only the most succulent melons, but also delicious gourds and fruits of every variety and colour. But you must never attempt to prune the vine or do anything to it other than gather the produce it yields. Do exactly as I say and you will never be short of food.'

Again Sebgugugu thanked the High God and promised to behave as he had been commanded. He quickly found the vine, watered it, and ordered his wife to harvest the fruit and vegetables it yielded. That evening, Sebgugugu sat down to a large helping of the wholesome food, and while his wife and children stood by, waiting to take their share of whatever he left behind, he patted his stomach contentedly and smiled at his good fortune.

But after a few weeks the same pattern repeated itself, and for no good reason, Sebgugugu became fidgety and began looking around him for some sort of diversion. Stooping to examine the vine one morning, he decided that it would be a far more productive plant if only its branches were thinned out to produce healthier shoots. He took his knife and without consulting anyone, began hacking at the stalks. But almost immediately, the vine withered away into the earth like a sun-scorched seedling.

Opposite: 'I have wasted the entire day waiting for that rock to deliver the food,' Sebgugugu declared. 'I am going to find a way to widen those cracks.'

This time when Imana appeared before Sebgugugu, he was fuming with anger. Sebgugugu fell on his knees and begged for forgiveness, but the High God spoke sternly, his voice as loud as the fiercest thunder:

'I have watched you disobey me repeatedly without any show of remorse,' he yelled, 'and it is only for the sake of your honest wife and

children that I am prepared to give you a third and final chance. Leave this place now and a little further down the road you will come across a large rock embedded in the soil. The rock will provide you with every kind of food – corn, milk, beans and other grains. Never attempt to force the food from the rock. Be patient and you will always be given as much as you need.'

Sebgugugu stood up, his heart pounding in his breast, and scuttled off in search of the rock, taking with him a basket and a jar. He soon reached the spot Imana had described and saw before him an enormous grey boulder. Moving closer to inspect it, he observed that its surface was covered in a number of small cracks. He held up his jar and at once, through the cracks, a thin stream of milk began to flow, followed by a long, steady line of corn. He carried this food back home to his family and they all sat down together to enjoy a very pleasant meal.

It seemed as if Sebgugugu had thoroughly mended his ways and for several months after the High God had admonished him, he remained an attentive and considerate husband and father. But one morning he awoke in a very bad mood, for his wife had taken ill, and now the responsibility of feeding and caring for the family fell on his shoulders alone. Sebgugugu set off towards the rock, but as he stood waiting for the milk to flow and the grain to appear, he became very impatient and kicked the rock furiously. By sunset, when he had finally gathered all he needed, his anger had multiplied tenfold, and he shouted in exasperation to his sick wife:

'I have wasted the entire day waiting for that rock to deliver the food. I can stand it no longer. I am going to find a way to widen those cracks no matter what it takes.'

And with his usual disregard for the welfare of his wife and family, Sebgugugu stormed outside where he cut some stout poles and hardened them in the fire.

Next morning, he returned to the rock, and using the great poles as levers, attempted to enlarge the cracks. The task was far easier than he had imagined and soon he had created a wide gap, large enough for him to pop his head through to take a closer look at the food. He pushed his nose towards the opening, but as he did so he was sucked further and further inwards until, with a crash like thunder, the gap closed up and the cracks disappeared, leaving not even the slightest trace on the smooth surface of the rock.

Sebgugugu's wife did not mourn his disappearance for very long and within a few months she had married a modest and respectable man from a neighbouring village. And if ever her children asked about their father, she told them the story of the glutton, who had pushed Imana's patience to the limit and had met with his just reward.

¹ Imana is the name given to the High God of the Bantu people, who commands everything, even Death.

The Feast

(From the Cameroon, west Africa)

ONCE THERE LIVED a kind and generous chief who wished to repay his people for the long hours they had worked for him on his farm. An idea came to him that he should hold a great feast and so he sent messengers to all of the surrounding villages inviting the men, women and children to attend his home the following evening, asking only that each man bring a calabash of wine along to the celebrations.

Next day, there was great excitement among the people. They chatted noisily about the event as they worked in the fields and when they had finished their labour they returned home to bathe and dress themselves in their finest robes. By sunset, more than a hundred men and their families lined the roadside. They laughed happily as they moved along, beating their drums and dancing in time to the rhythm. When they arrived at the chief's compound, the head of every household emptied his calabash into a large earthenware pot that stood in the centre of the courtyard. Soon the pot was more than half full and they all looked forward to their fair share of the refreshing liquid.

Among the chief's subjects there was a poor man who very much wanted to attend the feast, but he had no wine to take to the festivities and was too proud to appear empty-handed before his friends.

'Why don't you buy some wine from our neighbour?' his wife asked him, 'he looks as though he has plenty to spare.'

'But why should we spend money on a feast that is free?' the poor man answered her. 'No, there must be another way.'

And after he had thought about it hard for a few minutes he turned to his wife and said:

'There will be a great many people attending this feast, each of them carrying a calabash of wine. I'm sure that if I added to the pot just one calabash of water, nobody would notice the difference.'

His wife was most impressed by this plan, and while her husband went and filled his calabash with water, she stepped indoors and put on her best tunic and what little jewellery she possessed, delighted at the prospect of a good meal and an evening's free entertainment.

When the couple arrived at the chief's house they saw all the other guests empty the wine they had brought into the large earthen pot. The poor man moved forward nervously and followed their example. Then he went to where the men were gathered and sat down with them to await the serving of the wine.

As soon as the chief was satisfied that all the guests had arrived, he gave the order for his servants to begin filling everyone's bowl. The vessels were filled and the men looked to their host for the signal to begin the drinking. The poor man grew impatient, for he was quite desperate to have the taste of the wine on his lips, and could scarcely remember when he had last enjoyed such a pleasant experience for free.

At length, the chief stood up and delivered a toast to his people. Then he called for his guests to raise their bowls to their lips. Each of them tasted their wine, swallowed it, and waited to feel a warm glow inside.

They swallowed some more of the wine, allowing it to trickle slowly over their tongues, and waited for the flavour to release itself. But the wine tasted as plain as any water. And now, all around the room, the guests began to shuffle their feet and cough with embarrassment.

'This is really very good wine,' one of the men spoke up eventually.

'Indeed it is the best I've ever tasted,' agreed another.

'Quite the finest harvest I've ever come across,' added his neighbour.

But the chief of the people knew precisely what had happened, and he smiled at the comical spectacle as each man tried to hide the fact that he had filled his calabash that morning from the village spring.

The enormous earthen pot contained nothing but water, and it was water that the people were given to drink at the chief's great feast. For the chief had very wisely decided in his own mind:

'When only water is brought to the feast, water is all that should be served.'

Opposite: The people chatted noisily about the feast as they worked in the fields. When they finished their labour they returned home to dress in their finest robes.

The Three Tests

(From the Swahili speaking peoples, east Africa)

THERE ONCE LIVED A KING who had seven strong sons. When the day arrived for the eldest of them to leave the family home, he explained to his father that he longed to travel to a distant land and requested a sailing boat, together with some food and money. The king provided him with these things and the young man set sail across the ocean, promising to return to his family as soon as he had completed his great adventure.

He had been on the seas for some weeks when he spotted an island up ahead, and as he wished to rest awhile on dry land, he moored his boat and swam ashore. He found it a very pleasant spot, and strolled happily among the fruit-trees, helping himself to large handfuls of the juicy berries hanging from almost every branch. The berries satisfied not only his hunger, but also his thirst, and when the young man spat out the seeds, he noticed that they transformed themselves instantly into new plants laden with deliciously ripe fruit. Delighted with this discovery, he collected several baskets of the berries and took them on board his boat. He drew up his anchor and set sail once more, hoping that the next stage of his voyage would prove just as rewarding.

After several more days at sea, he approached another strange land, this time populated by a race of tall and powerful men, and discovered that it was ruled by a great sultan. Wishing to make a favourable impression, the young man offered the sultan some of the wonderful berries he had gathered, explaining how the seeds could bear fruit as soon as they touched fertile soil. The sultan was immediately suspicious and refused to believe a word until he had seen the evidence with his own eyes.

'If what you say is true,' the sultan declared, 'I will reward you handsomely. But if I find that you are lying, I will throw you in prison for having wasted my time.'

So the young man brought a basket of fruit from his boat, ate some of it and spat the seeds upon the ground. But to his great disappointment, the seeds lay there without altering their shape in any way. The sultan gave the signal, and at once a group of guards seized the young man, bound him, and carried him away to prison, promising that he would never again see the light of day.

When six months had passed and the king had still not received word of his eldest son, he began to grow extremely worried.

Opposite:
The king listened to his eldest son's request to travel to a distant land and provided him with a sailing boat, together with some food and money.

Ottimme Bushan 9?

His brothers were also very concerned for his safety and so it was agreed that the next eldest should go in search of him. It was not long before he, too, arrived on the island bearing the wonderful fruit-trees and when he had eaten some of the fruit and found that the seeds sprang to life as soon as they touched the soil, he gathered several baskets of the berries and took them on board his boat.

Shortly afterwards, the second son approached the sultan's kingdom and, as his brother had done before him, he began to boast of the miraculous fruit he had discovered, offering to demonstrate its remarkable magic to the sultan. He ate some of the berries and threw the seeds upon the ground. But the seeds failed to spring up, and the sultan, enraged that he had been made to look a fool a second time, immediately ordered him to be imprisoned in a chamber next to his eldest brother.

One by one, the king's sons set sail from the palace. Each landed on the island and gathered the enchanted berries. Each boasted of their wonderful magic when they arrived in the sultan's kingdom, and each was immediately thrown into prison when the seeds failed to sprout.

At last, only the youngest son remained. The boy's name was Sadaka, and although he was scarcely a youth, he could not be persuaded to abandon the thought of going in search of his brothers. The king eventually agreed to give him a boat and when he had loaded it with millet, rice and cattle, he embraced his mother and his father and took to the waves.

After a long, storm-tossed journey, Sadaka arrived on a cold, desolate island and climbed ashore hoping to find some trace of his brothers. But the first sight to greet him was a flock of weather-beaten birds, perilously close to starvation. Without any hesitation, the young boy hauled a sack of millet ashore and scattered it all around for the dying creatures to feed on. Soon the birds had recovered their strength, and in return for Sadaka's kindness, they begged him to accept from them an incense stick:

'Burn this stick if at any time you need us,' they told him, 'and we will smell it and come to help you.'

Sadaka accepted the gift and walked on towards the trees. He had not gone very far before he encountered a swarm of flies, weak with hunger and unable to take to the air. The boy immediately slaughtered the cattle he had on board and threw them on to the island. Soon the flies were buzzing around him gratefully. Their leader thanked Sadaka and gave him a second incense stick:

'If at any time you need us,' the flies told him, 'burn this stick and we will come to your aid.'

Sadaka explored a little further. Eventually he came upon a family of jinns who were also without food. He stopped to light a great fire and began cooking a large pot of rice for them to eat. The jinns marvelled at this generosity and when they had eaten their fill, they handed him an incense stick, identical to the other two, instructing him to burn it if ever he ran into trouble.

Sadaka sailed away and before he had even lost sight of the island, the sun began to shine, the sea grew calmer, and soon he had arrived at the place where his brothers had gathered the enchanted berries. He could not quite believe his eyes when the seeds he spat out blossomed into new trees, and so he decided to gather some of the fruit and take it to the jinns to show them.

'O yes,' said the sultan of the jinns, 'we have heard all about these berries and they are very real. But if you intend to show them to anyone else, it is important to know that the miracle will only happen when the seeds fall on special soil.'

The young boy considered this information for a time, then he thanked the jinns and returned to the island of the fruit trees. Here he gathered up enough of the precious soil to fill three wooden barrels. He rolled the barrels on to his boat, hoisted his sails and set out to sea once more.

After he had travelled only a short stretch of the ocean he came upon the sultan's kingdom and presented himself before the great ruler.

'I have journeyed here in search of my brothers,' he informed the sultan, 'and if any of your people can help me find them, I will reward them with a very special tree that will always bear more fruit than they can eat, and whose branches will always remain strong and productive even in times of famine.'

But the sultan laughed uproariously for some minutes at the young man's speech.

'Listen to this fool,' he called to his attendants. 'There are six men in my prison who came here boasting exactly the same thing. See to it that this one joins them.'

But Sadaka began to protest noisily:

'Give me a chance to prove myself,' he pleaded. 'Tomorrow I will show you this wonder, but please be patient with me until then.'

'So be it,' replied the sultan indifferently, 'but remember, if you fail, I will show no mercy and you will be cast into prison with the others.'

That night, when he was certain that everyone lay sleeping , Sadaka crept from his chamber and headed towards the shore. He dragged the first of the three barrels from his boat and began sprinkling the soil thinly and evenly upon the ground. The work took several long hours and he had only just emptied the last of the barrels when the first rays of sunshine peered over the horizon. Silently and carefully, he crawled back to his bed and waited there anxiously for the people to stir.

As soon as the sultan and the wise men of the kingdom had awoken, Sadaka was summoned to appear before him. He carried a small basket of fruit with him and set it down on the ground. Slowly he lifted a handful of the ripe berries and began chewing on them. The sultan yawned aloud and twisted in his seat. The wise men glanced around them and took very little notice. But when Sadaka spat the seeds upon the earth and they began to rise up before their eyes, the sultan and all the people on the island cried out in sheer delight. Again Sadaka performed his great miracle and soon he was joined by others who ate the fruit and spat out the seeds until the whole kingdom blossomed with the magic trees.

From that moment onwards, the sultan took Sadaka under his wing and saw to it that everything he needed was provided for him. Almost immediately, he arranged for his brothers to be released from prison and ordered a great feast to be held to celebrate their freedom. And as time moved on, the sultan grew very fond of the young man and wished that he had been blessed with an equally wise and generous son of his own.

The sultan possessed a daughter, however, whose extraordinary beauty and talent were famous throughout the land. It was not long before Sadaka came to hear of her many virtues and when, one day, he spotted her strolling through the palace gardens, his heart was filled with a deep desire to be with her. He went before the sultan and asked if he might make her his wife, but to his surprise, the sultan grew very angry and declared that he had yet to encounter a man even half good enough to marry his daughter.

'What would I have to do to prove my worth to you?' Sadaka asked him, 'I will do anything you ask, for now that I have seen her, my heart will never be at peace.'

Opposite: Although Sadaka was scarcely a youth, he could not be persuaded to abandon the thought of taking to the ocean in search of his older brothers.

The sultan led Sadaka to a very large storeroom and pointed to the hundreds of sacks containing all kinds of mixed grain.

'If you can separate these different kinds of grain and place each kind in its own sack by tomorrow morning, then you may marry the

princess,' he announced.

Sadaka eyes widened in disbelief at the sight of the huge task facing him, but he so badly wanted the sultan's daughter, he agreed at least to try his hand. So he sat down on the floor and began sorting through the first sack. But after a very short time, he realized how hopeless the situation was and buried his head in his hands. Then he suddenly remembered the incense stick the birds on the lonely island had given him. He took the stick from beneath his robe, and as soon as the pungent odour filled the air, a flock of birds appeared out of nowhere asking what they might do to help him. After the birds had heard what the sultan had ordered, they flew around the room and began picking up the grain in their beaks, separating each kind into its own sack.

Next morning, when the sultan arrived at his storehouse, he saw that all the grain was separated as he had ordered. But he walked away, shaking his head and gathered his wise men around him. At length, he came and spoke to Sadaka:

'We cannot quite believe what we have seen,' he told the young man, 'and so you must prove yourself once more if you wish to marry my daughter. If you can cut through the trunk of that Baobab tree over there, with one stroke of your sword, you can take her.'

Sadaka saw that the tree was of an enormous size and knew that he could not possibly perform what was required of him without help. So he asked to be allowed to go back to his room to get his weapon and here he burned the second incense stick. At once the family of jinns appeared before him and when he told them what the sultan wanted him to do, they flew away and returned with an army of white ants that marched towards the tree. The ants gnawed at the trunk leaving only the bark so that when Sadaka approached and drew his sword, he easily cut the tree in half and it fell to the ground effortlessly.

But the sultan was still not satisfied:

'Tomorrow will be your final test,' he told Sadaka. 'In the afternoon all the maidens of the kingdom will pass in front of you one by one, each of them wearing identical veils over their faces. You must pick the princess from among them and if you choose correctly, you shall have her for your wife.'

Then Sadaka retired once more to his chamber and burnt his last incense stick. Immediately, the leader of the flies appeared and Sadaka explained what had been demanded of him.

'When the maidens of the city pass before you,' said the fly, 'I will stand in front of you and you must keep watch on me. When the princess draws near, I will drum my wings and alight on her shoulder as she passes by.'

So the next afternoon all the maidens of the kingdom passed in a procession before the sultan and his attendants and, as promised, the leader of the flies took to the air and landed on the shoulder of the princess as she walked past. Sadaka stood up and walked forward to where the princess stood, planting a kiss on her cheek for everyone around to see.

Sadaka had now passed his three tests and the sultan could not deny he was more than a fitting son-in-law. Proudly he took the princess by the arm and led her away. They were married the very next day and the sultan built for them a fine palace where they lived a long and happy life together.

The Two Rogues

(From the Hausa speaking peoples, west Africa)

AMONG THE HAUSA PEOPLE, there were two men, each as devious as the other, who spent most of their time plotting and planning how best to earn a living by dishonest means. One rogue lived in Kano, while the other lived in Katsina, and although they had never actually met, news of their trickery travelled back and forth between the villages, so that even with some distance between them, they considered themselves powerful rivals.

One morning, when the rogue from Kano had run rather short of money, he sat down by a palm tree to consider his next crooked scheme. Suddenly an idea came to him and, taking his hunting knife, he began peeling a long length of bark from the tree. After he had trimmed it carefully, he took it to one of the women at the dye-pit and asked her to dip it in blue ink for him. The wood looked impressive when it had been stained, but in order to improve it even more, the rogue from Kano painted it with a glaze, giving it the appearance of the finest blue broadcloth. Then he wrapped it up in paper, placed it in his leather bag and set out for market, confident that the cloth would fetch a very favourable price.

But while the rogue from Kano had been doing all of this, the rogue from Katsina had also kept himself busy, for he, too, had recently run short of funds and had only a couple of hundred cowries left to his name. So he took a goatskin, laid it flat on the ground and heaped several loads of pebbles on to it. Then he sprinkled the cowries on top, drew the four corners together and set off with his bundle to market.

Half way along the road, the two rogues happened to meet and soon fell into conversation as they walked along.

'Where are you off to, my friend?' asked the rogue from Kano.

'I'm on my way to market,' said the rogue from Katsina. 'I've got all my money here in cowries, twenty thousand of them, and I intend to purchase something very special for my wife.'

'Well, fancy that! I was just heading in the same direction myself,' said the rogue from Kano, 'and I have with me the very best blue broadcloth to sell to the highest bidder.'

'Wouldn't it be nice to avoid such a long journey in this heat,' said the rogue from Katsina. 'You look almost as weary as I feel and we still have exactly the same distance to go.'

And so the two men rapidly abandoned all thought of going to market. They struck a bargain on the spot and exchanged their wares before parting in great friendship, each one believing he had got the better of the other.

When they had moved off a short distance, each man stopped in his path to examine the bargain he had carried away. But, of course, the rogue from Kano discovered that he had been handed a bag of stones, while the rogue from Katsina found that he had purchased little more than a parcel of bark.

As soon as they discovered they had been duped, they each turned back and retraced their steps until eventually they came face to face once more. At first angry and belligerent, they soon realized they had much in common and grew calmer at the thought of putting this to lucrative use:

'We are each as crafty as the other,' they said, 'and it would be wisest from now on to join forces and seek our fortune together.'

Shaking hands on this arrangement, they took to the road without further hostility and walked on until they had arrived at a neighbouring town. Here they found an old woman who sold them water-bottles, staffs and begging-bowls, and when they had equipped themselves with these items, they set off once more, pretending to be blind beggars as they hobbled along in the afternoon sunshine.

Opposite: One rogue lived in Kano, while the other lived in Katsina. They had never actually met, but news of their trickery travelled between the villages.

They followed a dusty trail deep into the bush and before long stumbled upon a party of traders pitching camp among the trees. The traders had only just begun to unload their caravan and as the two rogues hid in the undergrowth feasting their eyes on the rich cargo, they began

discussing a plan which would enable them to get their hands on as much of the goods as possible.

Later that evening, when darkness had descended upon the camp, the two rogues came out of hiding and moved slowly towards the fire where the traders had just gathered together for their evening meal, beating their staffs on the ground before them and squeezing their eyes tightly shut. The pitiful sight they presented earned them immediate sympathy and without delay they were handed platefuls of hot food and encouraged to spend the night at the camp.

Soon the traders retired to their beds accompanied by the blind men who complained aloud of the great weariness that had suddenly overtaken them. They pretended to be the very first to fall asleep, but as soon as they were certain everyone else had followed their example, they opened their eyes again and crept from their beds. Very quietly, they began to rummage through the traders' property, carrying off quantities of food, drink, precious jewellery and money to a dry well a short distance away into which they very carefully dropped them.

Next morning when the party awoke and found they had been robbed of everything, they were quite devastated and began an immediate search for the thieves. The two rogues did not escape suspicion, but having anticipated that their innocence might be questioned, they had already made certain that some of their own possessions had been carried off.

'Where are our water-bottles?' they cried out in mock-despair, 'and our staffs! They are missing also. How will we manage to walk without them?'

But the traders grew angry to hear them voice such petty concerns.

'Here we are,' they cried, 'robbed of everything we own, and all you miserable beggars can think about are your water-bottles and your walking sticks. Get out of here before we throw you out.'

But as they groped their way through the bush, the two rogues smiled at one another, knowing that as soon as the coast was clear, they would hurry off to the well and help themselves to the stolen goods.

'Why don't you go down into the well,' said the rogue from Kano to his companion. 'I have strong labourer's hands and I can use a rope to haul up the goods more skilfully than you.'

'No, you go down,' said the rogue from Katsina, 'I have much better eyesight and can keep a more careful watch up here in case any of the traders return.'

'No, you go,' said the rogue from Kano.

'No, you,' replied the rogue from Katsina.

And they continued to argue back and forth in this manner for several minutes until, finally, the rogue from Katsina reluctantly agreed to go down into the well. Soon his companion had lowered a strong rope to which he tied the goods, allowing them to be hauled to the top swiftly and smoothly. The rogue from Kano worked as quickly as possible above the surface, trying hard to conceal the fact that while he stacked the stolen goods, he was also gathering together a mound of boulders at the mouth of the well. But his companion below had a pretty shrewd idea of what the rogue from Kano intended for him and was resolved to keep his head about him at all times.

When, at long last, the work of retrieving the stolen property had almost come to an end, the rogue from Kano shouted into the well:

'My friend, when you have secured the last item to the rope and are ready to come up yourself, give me a shout. That way, I can haul you up very carefully so that you don't tear yourself on the jagged stones along the sides.'

But the rogue from Katsina did not trust this gesture of friendship and shouted back:

'The next load will be a pretty heavy one, but it is the only thing left down here.'

Then he crawled into the last of the bales of wheat and hid himself inside.

The rogue from Kano now hauled up the remaining bale and carried it over to where he had stacked the other goods, not suspecting for one moment that his companion lay concealed within it. He then walked to the mouth of the well and began hurling the boulders into the opening one by one until he was satisfied that he had completely covered the base and crushed anything resting at the bottom.

But while he was busy doing this, the rogue from Katsina crawled out of hiding and started to divide up the stolen property, placing some in the bushes, some underneath the rocks and some beneath his robes. The hoard had been reduced to little or nothing by the time he heard his companion walking back from the well. He had no wish to be discovered alive, and so he decided to retreat to the bush until nightfall, at which time he intended to return and gather up everything for himself alone.

The rogue from Kano scratched his head in dismay and sat down on the ground trying to solve the riddle of the missing goods he had so carefully stacked by the side of the well.

'Someone must have come in the last few minutes and taken the stuff away,' he exclaimed to himself, but then it occurred to him that the thief could not be very far away and that, in all probability, he would be in desperate need of

a pack-horse to help him carry his load.

The thought had no sooner entered his head when he leaped into the shelter of the trees and began braying like a donkey. Sure enough, after a few minutes, he saw a figure hurrying towards him calling out:

'Steady there donkey! Hold on until I can get to you. Don't run away now, boy!'

The figure reached through the branches and seized him by the collar. Within seconds, the rogue from Kano found himself pinned to the ground staring into the eyes of the rogue from Katsina. The two men remained speechless for a time, but then they stood up, smiled knowingly at one another and began dusting down their clothes.

Silently, they gathered up their booty and continued on their travels once more. The road they now followed happened to take them past the rogue of Kano's house and here the two men sat down and finally divided up the stolen property fairly and squarely.

Some days later, however, the rogue of Katsina announced his wish to visit his own family.

'I cannot possibly carry my share of the goods with me,' he told his companion, 'but I will leave them here and in three months' time I will come back and collect what is mine.'

And so he set off, believing he had seen the last of his friend's trickery and that he had nothing more to fear.

Two months passed by and the rogue of Kano kept his word and never once laid a finger on his friend's share of the stolen property. But when the third month had almost come to an end, he ordered his family to dig a grave in the field close to their hut. Then, on the night before the rogue of Katsina was due to return, he gathered up all of the goods, including his friend's portion, crammed them into a sack, and threw them into the grave, instructing his family to bury him alive alongside them.

'Cover the grave over with fresh earth,' he told his family, 'and when Katsina returns, say that I have passed away and that you have buried the contents of the house with me.'

And so, next morning, as soon as the family saw the rogue from Katsina appear in the distance, they ran towards him weeping and wailing:

'You have arrived too late!' they cried. 'Our brother is dead. We buried him four days ago.'

'Really?' said the rogue from Katsina, rather taken aback by the news. 'So he has gone the way of all flesh and taken his most valuable

Opposite:
The two men remained speechless for a time, but then they stood up, smiled knowingly at one another and began dusting down their clothes.

possessions with him, I suppose.'

'O yes!' replied the family, 'everything was cast into the grave, for we were uncertain which items belonged to him.'

'Take me to the grave so that I may see this for myself,' said the rogue from Katsina, his suspicion increasing every moment. 'I must pay my last respects even if I have missed out on the burial.'

When he was taken to the grave the rogue from Katsina broke into loud lamentations, but after a few minutes, when he had recovered himself, he spoke to the family:

'You really ought to cut some thorn-bushes and cover the mound well,' he told them, 'otherwise the hyenas may come and dig up the body and scatter the bones.'

'We'll do it tomorrow,' promised the family, and saying this, they led the rogue of Katsina into their hut and provided him with supper and a comfortable bed for the night.

At the first sign of darkness, when the household had grown very quiet, the rogue from Katsina stole from his bed and walked to his friend's grave. He crouched to the ground and began to growl ferociously, dropping on his hands and knees and scrabbling at the earth as if he were a hyena trying to get at the corpse underneath.

Inside the grave the rogue from Kano awoke from his sleep, and as soon as he heard the loud scratching and growling sounds he screamed out in terror:

'Help, help! Someone save me! The hyenas have come for me. They are trying to eat me. Let me out of here!'

The rogue from Katsina continued to dig, until he caught sight of his friend's ghostly face, lifted towards the opening in sheer horror.

'All right,' he said, 'out you come, Kano. I think you have finally learned your lesson.'

The rogue from Kano seized his friend's hand and was lifted to the surface. He was more relieved to see the rogue from Katsina than he had ever believed possible and as it began to dawn on him, once and for all, that he had finally met his match, he suddenly burst into a fit of laughter:

'Katsina, you are a scoundrel,' he said as he tittered away to himself.

'Yes, and you are another!' Katsina replied smiling from ear to ear.

✳   ✳   ✳

Further Reading

Abrahams, Roger D., *African Folklore*, (New York: Pantheon Books, 1983) • Arnott, Kathleen, *African Myths and Legends*, (Oxford University Press, 1962) • Barker, W.H. and Sinclair, C., *West African Folk Tales*, (London: George Harrap & Co and Sheldon Press, 1917) • Cardinall, A.W., *Tales Told in Togoland*, (Oxford University Press, 1931) • Courlander, Harold, *A Treasury of African Folklore*, (New York: Marlowe & Company, 1996) • Courlander, Harold, *The Crest and the Hide and Other African Stories*, (London: Victor Gollancz Ltd, 1984) • Dayrell, Elphinstone, *Folk Stories from Southern Nigeria*, (London, 1910) • Finnigan, Rugh, *Oral Literature in Africa*, (Oxford: The Clarendon Press, 1970) • Fox, D.C., and Frobenius, Leo, *African Genesis*, (New York: Stackpole Sons, 1937) • Johnston, H.A.S., *A Selection of Hausa Stories*, (Oxford: The Clarendon Press, 1966) • Knappert, Jan, *Fables from Africa*, (London: Evans Brothers Ltd, 1980) • Knappert, Jan, *Myths and Legends of the Swahili*, (London: Heinemann, 1970) • Mbiti, John S., *Akamba Stories*, (Oxford: The Clarendon Press, 1966) Parinder, Geoffrey, *African Mythology*, (London: Paul Hamlyn, 1967) • Torrend, S.J., *Specimens of Bantu Folklore*, (London: Kegan Paul, Trench, Trubner & Co Ltd, 1921) • Werner, Alice, *African Myths and Legends*, (London: George Harrap & Co, 1933)

Notes on Illustrations

Page 5 Detail from *On the Bank of an African River*, by Briton Riviere (Guildhall Art Gallery, Corporation of London). Courtesy of The Bridgeman Art Library. **Page 7** *Near Sidbury, Cape Province*, by Thomas Baines (Royal Geographical Society, London). Courtesy of The Bridgeman Art Library. **Page 9** *An Eastern Street Scene*, by Walter R. I. Tyndale (Chris Beetles Ltd., London). Courtesy of The Bridgeman Art Library. **Page 11** Detail from *Buffaloes Driven to the Edge of the Chasm Opposite Garden Island, Victoria Falls*, by Thomas Baines (Royal Geographical Society, London). Courtesy of The Bridgeman Art Library. **Page 15** *Native Boat Between Sierra Leone and Adjacent Country*, by Thomas Baines (Royal Geographical Society, London). Courtesy of The Bridgeman Art Library. **Page 17** Detail from *Meeting with Hostile Natives*, by Thomas Baines (Royal Geographical Society, London). Courtesy of The Bridgeman Art Library. **Page 19** Detail from *Monitors*, by P. J. Smit. Courtesy of The Mary Evans Picture Library. **Page 20** Detail from *Three Channel Rapids Above Kebrabasa on the Zambezi*, by Thomas Baines (Royal Geographical Society, London). Courtesy of The Bridgeman Art Library. **Page 23** Detail from *Victoria Falls with Stampeding Buffalo*, by Thomas Baines (Royal Geographical Society, London). Courtesy of The Bridgeman Art Library. **Page 24** Detail from *Victoria Falls with Stampeding Buffalo*, by Thomas Baines (Royal Geographical Society, London). Courtesy of The Bridgeman Art Library. **Page 27** *Clearing in the Forest*, by Caspar-David Friedrich (Neue Galerie, Linz). Courtesy of The Bridgeman Art Library. **Pages 29** Detail from *A Moonlit Lake by a Castle*, by Joseph Wright of Derby (Christie's, London). Courtesy of The Bridgeman Art Library. **Page 30** Detail from *The Great Western Fall, Victoria Falls*, by Thomas Baines (Royal Geographical Society, London). Courtesy of The Bridgeman Art Library. **Page 33** *Shibante, a Native of Mazaro, Boatman and Pilot Belonging to Major Second*, by Thomas Baines (Royal Geographical Society, London). Courtesy of The Bridgeman Art Library. **Page 36** Detail from *Meeting with Hostile Natives*, by Thomas Baines (Royal Geographical Society, London). Courtesy of The Bridgeman Art Library. **Page 39** *Nubier*, by Friedrich Ratzel (Die Kulturvolker der Alten und Neuen Welt, Leipzig). Courtesy of AKG Photo. **Page 41** *Victoria Falls of the Zambezi River*, by Thomas Baines (Royal Geographical Society.) Courtesy of The Bridgeman Art Library. **Page 43** Detail from *On the Bank of an African River*, by Briton Riviere (Guildhall Art Gallery, Corporation of London). Courtesy of The Bridgeman Art Library. **Page 45** Detail from *Spiders and Snakes*, by Albert Seba (Private Collection). Courtesy of The Bridgeman Art Library. **Page 46** Detail from *Spiders and Snakes*, by Albert Seba (Private Collection). Courtesy of The Bridgeman Art Library. **Page 51** *Spiders (Mygole) from "Over de Voorteeling", Plate 18*, by Marie Sybille Merian (Victoria and Albert Museum, London). Courtesy of The Bridgeman Art Library. **Page 59** Detail from *Prehistoric Encounter*, by Tirzah Ravilious (Private Collection). Courtesy of The Bridgeman Art Library. **Page 60** Detail from *The Great Western Fall, Victoria Falls*, by Thomas Baines (Royal Geographical Society, London). Courtesy of The Bridgeman Art Library. **Page 63** *Baboons*. Courtesy of The Mary Evans Picture Library. **Page 67** *Soft River Tortoises* by P. J. Smit. Courtesy of The Mary Evans Picture Library. **Page 71** Detail from *Mud Hole African Elephants*, by Eric Forlee (Eaton Gallery, London). Courtesy of The Bridgeman Art Library. **Page 73** *The Leopard*, by John Sargent Noble (David Messum Gallery, London). Courtesy of The Bridgeman Art Library. **Page 74** *A Lion Amongst Scrub*, by Arthur Wardle (Bonhams, London). Courtesy of The Bridgeman Art Library. **Page 77** Detail from *On the Bank of an African River*, by Briton Riviere (Guildhall Art Gallery, Corporation of London). Courtesy of The Bridgeman Art Library. **Page 80** *The Snake Charmer*, by Henri J. F. Rousseau (Musee National D'Art Moderne, Paris). Courtesy of The Bridgeman Art Library. **Page 83** *Part of the Tete Looking up the Zambezi from Ruins*, by Thomas Baines (Royal Geographical Society, London). Courtesy of The Bridgeman Art Library. **Page 91** *The Black Iguana*, by P. J. Smit. Courtesy of The Mary Evans Picture Library. **Page 93** *Conde - A Native of Tete*, by Thomas Baines (Royal Geographical Society, London). Courtesy of The Bridgeman Art Library. **Page 99** *Amara of Janna in the Mandingo Country*, by Thomas Baines (Royal Geographical Society, London). Courtesy of The Bridgeman Art Library. **Page 102** *Mountain Scene*, by William Gersham Collingwood (Royal Watercolour Society, London). Courtesy of The Bridgeman Art Libary. **Page 106** *Peter Falta, Mandingo Man*, by Thomas Baines (Royal Geographical Society, London). Courtesy of The Bridgeman Art Library. **Page 110** *Working on a Coal Seam Near Tete*, by Thomas Baines (Royal Geographical Society, London). Courtesy of The Bridgeman Art Library. **Page 113** *Utimuni, Nephew of Shaka, the Zulu Warrior King*, by George French Angas (Private Collection). Courtesy of The Bridgeman Art Library. **Page 117** *Town of Tete from the North Shore of the Zambesi*, by Thomas Baines (Royal Geographical Society, London). Courtesy of The Bridgeman Art Library. **Page 121** Painting courtesy of The Foundry Creative Media Company Ltd, after *Kaffer und Botswana*, by W. Adams. **Page 124** Painting courtesy of The Foundry Creative Media Company Ltd, after *Kaffer und Botswana*, by W. Adams.

Index